Sales people say...

"This book offers a refreshing approach to classic sales problems, and **belongs in every sales library**. It will help experienced sales people to come up with new ideas for selling, by combining their specialized product knowledge with advertising principles that have proven their value for more than 100 years." – Larry Wilson, author, *The One Minute Sales Person* and *Play to Win*

"This book shows you how to use the most practical, proven techniques of advertising to **make more sales, faster than ever before.**" – Brian Tracy, author, *The Psychology of Selling* and *Advanced Selling Strategies*

"Hassett takes the millions of dollars in research directed to advertising persuasion and applies it to practical and powerful techniques that compel people to buy. **Read this book!** The principles are priceless." – Robert E. Krumroy, author, *Identity Branding* and *Please...Make ME a Little Bit FAMOUS*

"Advertising is a sales engine that makes the economy hum. The success of advertising depends on its ability to attract attention, engage the customer, appeal to self interest and add value to a person's life. AdverSelling demonstrates that these principles are essential to successful face to face selling as well. By using advertising examples, Jim Hassett **makes the whole selling process new and vibrant again**. Even old pros will sit up and take notice. The ideas are fresh. The writing is vigorous, fun and filled with 'aha's'. Don't read this if you want to do things the same old way. But if you are willing to change and to improve, this book is for you." – Kevin Daley, author, *Talk Your Way to the Top* and *Socratic Selling*

"AdverSelling distills over a century of tested and proven marketing wisdom into 26 sure-fire rules every salesperson on Earth can use **dozens of times every day**. Short, hard-hitting and super-readable chapters make it easy and fast to spot just the right secret for ratcheting up your next phone call, e-mail, letter, proposal or presentation to be a winner. I say buy three copies so you always have one close at hand in the office, at home and in your car." – Don Schrello, author, *The Complete Marketing Handbook For Consultants*

"The AdverSelling process made people write down their plans and try something new. We **accomplished more in a few hours with AdverSelling** than we had in several months of weekly sales meetings." – Dominic Sestito, Chief Operating Officer, Telamon Insurance Network

"The workshop quickly focused on specific, practical tasks to increase our sales effectiveness. We generated an action plan to improve product demonstrations and implemented it over the next few weeks. We've seen an **immediate improvement** in the quality of our presentations and have no doubt that this will lead to **increased sales**." – Martin Cook, Sales Manager for the Americas, Wall Street Systems

ʼed the **practical applications** that this workshop
ʼled." – John Egan, Investment Consultant, TD
ʼhouse

ʼrkshop produced **immediate and practical**
ʼot an idea for a new customer information survey.
ʼa template within a few days, and now use it to
ʼat we address the individual needs of every new
ʼstomer." – Dianne M. Holland, Sales Manager
ʼn, Verizon

ʼorks." – Edward J. O'Donnell, Division
ʼRetail and Small Business Services, The

AdverSelling™

How to build stronger relationships and close more sales by applying 26 principles from successful advertising campaigns.

James Hassett, Ph.D.

www.advertraining.com

800-49-TRAIN

Published by

The Advertraining® Group, Inc.
800-49-TRAIN
www.advertraining.com

Cover design by Ginny Weaver, The Advertraining Group
Cover photo copyright © ArtToday, Inc.
Author photo by Bachrach

To Pat and Eileen.

They make me happy.

Table of contents

Preface

When I wrote this book, my company specialized in training and coaching professional sales people. Around the time it came out, my lawyer said to me: "You know who really needs sales training? Lawyers."

This casual comment led first to a series of projects with lawyers, and later to refocusing my company exclusively on the legal profession, and changing its name to LegalBizDev.

In all honesty, I thought this book would fade away, because it would be hard to find a word that is less appealing to lawyers than its title. AdverSelling combines two of their least favorite concepts – advertising and selling - in a single word. I put it on the shelf, next to the psychology textbooks I had written in my days in academia, and went on to write *Legal Business Development: A Step by Step Guide* and *The LegalBizDev Desk Reference*.

But a funny thing happened as LegalBizDev became more and more successful: sales of this book began to climb. So now we are reprinting it, with this new preface and an updated bio, but everything else unchanged.

In the preface for the first and second printings, I thanked many clients and colleagues who had reviewed drafts and made suggestions, including:

Commonwealth Financial	William P. Avril
Communispond	Kevin Daley
Economic Stabilization Trust	Robert Germino
Equation Partners	Alan Roy Hollander
New York Life Insurance	R. Morris Sims
Schrello Direct Marketing	Don M. Schrello
The Bank of New York	Gail Gross
	Ed O'Donnell
	Marva Webb
TD Waterhouse	Jeff Rossi
	Pamela Thalund
Telamon Insurance	Michael J. Susco
	Christopher J. DeLorey
	Sandra M. O'Neil
	Dominic F. Sestito
Verizon	Sean Gorman
	Dianne M. Holland
	Lewis Long
Wall Street Systems	Martin Cook
	Joe Patrina
	Rick Schumacher

If I ever decide to add a hundred pages to the preface, I can tell you a little about all the help they provided. But, at the risk of shortchanging the others, I must single out two people from this list.

Don Schrello is my mentor and my friend. Nearly a decade ago, I began studying his book *How to Market Training & Information*, still the best book in this field. I later hired Don as a consultant, and have been following his advice ever since. Don says that developing AdverSelling reminds him of his first job (with the Apollo space program, sending a man to the moon). He is still advising me today on LegalBizDev.

Rick Schumacher started as a client and later became a friend. The day I decided to begin work on AdverSelling, I first went to Rick's office to get his advice. Rick also participated in the second AdverSelling workshop, and read every word of an endless round of drafts. Of all of Rick's achievements, I personally am proudest of the fact that in the 2003 New York Marathon, he beat Sean Combs (then known as Puff Daddy, and now as Diddy).

And of course the list would not be complete without Pat, my wife, my anchor, my best friend. And without Pat, there would be no Eileen. I cannot imagine a world without Eileen. If I got to live my life over, I'd have to do everything the same for the first thirty-five years, just to make sure she was born.

Jim Hassett
January 2008

"If you don't sell,
it's not the product that's wrong, it's you."
– Estee Lauder

Introduction

How to get started

AdverSelling™ helps experienced sales people to increase productivity by applying twenty-six principles from successful advertising campaigns. AdverSelling is a research-based process that will produce immediate and practical results that fit your customers and your selling style.

For more than a hundred years, advertisers have discovered, tested, and refined powerful techniques to persuade people to buy. But most sales people – and their managers – don't use these principles consistently or fully benefit from their power.

Table 1 lists twenty-six AdverSelling principles that you can use to increase the effectiveness of every email you send, every phone call you make, and every meeting you attend.

Wait, you may say. I am already using these principles. Of course you are. Successful sales people apply them every day.

But this book and the AdverSelling process will help you to use these powerful principles more effectively, and get more out of them. Once you start using AdverSelling to generate new ideas that fit your product and your personal strengths, you will sell more.

Table 1
26 AdverSelling™ Principles

The top six
1   Attract attention
2   Engage your customers
3   Appeal to self-interest
4   Add value
5   Listen
6   Test early and often

Your attitude
7   Be optimistic and credible
8   Be creative
9   Stimulate curiosity
10   Ask for help
11   Build consensus

Your message
12   Personalize and customize
13   Quote testimonials
14   Use a slogan
15   Build on the brand
16   Repeat the message

Your presentations
17   Make a good first impression
18   Tell a story
19   Dramatize the dull
20   Write powerful headlines
21   Less is more

Your actions
22   Make people happy
23   Be cautious with humor
24   Require immediate action
25   Look good
26   Don't stop

Will it work for me?

AdverSelling will help any professional who has mastered the basics and is motivated to sell more. It is not for beginners. If you are looking for a book about basic selling skills, just go to Amazon, type in the term "sales training," and start working your way through fifty thousand titles.

The books you find will cover such skills as negotiation, listening, questioning, managing time and building relationships. Almost all include useful ideas.[1] But the more you already know about sales, the less these books will help you.

Paradoxically, this book is just the opposite: the more you know about selling already, the more it will help. That's because if you know more, the ideas you generate with AdverSelling are more likely to fit your customers and product, and they're more likely to increase sales.

We developed AdverSelling to fill a gap in the market. The world is full of successful sales people who would like to increase sales, but there were no books or procedures directly addressing this audience. Until now.

The reason behind the gap is that top producers need highly specialized information.

We can't tell you how to sell to your customers, because you know more about it than we do. But we can show you how to use AdverSelling principles to improve your focus, become more productive, and accomplish more with the knowledge you already have.

This book will create a synergy between your expertise about your product and your market, and our expertise in advertising and research.

Managers love AdverSelling, because it boosts productivity for top producers. And according to the 2004 Miller Heiman Sales Effectiveness Study, the biggest challenge sales teams face is "to accelerate the

productivity and effectiveness of talented people once
they're in the right positions."[2]

The Gallup organization has found that the top twenty-
five percent of a sales team typically sell four to ten times
as much as average performers. They also stay longer at
their companies, develop more loyal customers, and sign
business with better margins.[3] Therefore, from a
manager's point of view, a ten percent improvement for a
top sales person will produce far more revenue that a ten
percent improvement for a beginner.

But suppose your company already teaches a proprietary
approach to sales, or that you have adopted a particular
framework such as strategic selling or consultative
selling or SPIN selling or relationship selling. Will
AdverSelling require you to head in a new direction?

Not at all. AdverSelling is not designed to replace your
system, but rather to work with it. This book draws on
the lessons of each: SPIN selling in Chapter 4, strategic
selling in Chapter 11, consultative selling in Chapter 12,
and relationship selling in Chapter 26. AdverSelling will
help you decide when to draw on each of these powerful
methods.

Will it work for you? We've used these principles to
successfully train thousands of professionals over the last
nineteen years. Our web page has numerous testimonials
from satisfied customers.

But what do you care? You only care if AdverSelling
works in your business, for you. And so there's only one
way to find out: try it and see.

Four step process

AdverSelling helps experienced sales professionals
change behavior immediately, starting with tasks that
have the greatest impact. The process consists of four
steps:

Step 1: Identify opportunities to maximize impact. List the top opportunities to increase short-term sales productivity. Focus on tasks you could realistically accomplish in the next thirty days, such as getting more referrals or closing particular accounts.

Step 2: Brainstorm with 26 AdverSelling principles. Use the principles to generate a list of specific sales tactics aimed at these opportunities. In our workshops, we use a structured process of speed brainstorming for this step, with the goal of quickly generating as many ideas as possible.

Step 3: Define your AdverSelling activity. Select the best item from the brainstormed list. Then develop week by week AdverSelling activities that meet SMART criteria — they must be Specific, Measurable, Achievable, Relevant, and Timed.

Step 4: Test and improve. In the thirty days after the workshop, build on the things that work, improve the rest.

In our workshops, we fine tune these steps for each group, based on the people and products. But the process is so powerful that even if you decide to "do it yourself," you can shorten your sales cycle just by using this book.

Build on your strengths

AdverSelling™ is built on research, and nobody has done more research on sales than the Gallup organization. Over the last forty years, they've interviewed over twenty-five thousand sales managers, two hundred fifty thousand salespeople, and a million customers. In the book *Discover Your Sales Strengths*, Benson Smith and Tony Rutigliano summarized Gallup's conclusions with these three keys to sales success: "1) discover your strengths, 2) find the right fit, and 3) work for the right manager."[4]

If you've read the Gallup bestseller *Now, Discover Your Strengths* by Marcus Buckingham and Donald Clifton,[5] then you already know that people are most productive and happiest when they find a job that fits their personal talents. Maybe, like one million other people, you've even diagnosed your own top five talents from their thirty-four positive personality themes, including Empathy, Responsibility, Positivity, Competition, and Self-Assurance. Smith & Rutigliano's book explains how this model relates to sales.

According to an old cliché: "A good salesperson can sell anything." Gallup's data proves that is simply not true. In fact, top producers in one industry often perform poorly in another, because selling in different industries requires different skills: "The strengths that make someone an excellent pharmaceutical salesperson are different from those required to excel in selling real estate, or jet engines, or strategic consulting."[6] Just as Michael Jordan found that basketball skills did not help him get to first base, a sales star in one industry may do poorly in another.

Gallup also found that each successful salesperson develops a unique selling style based upon their particular personality strengths. In their surveys, one of the items best correlated to sales success is how highly people agree with this statement: "At work I get to do what I do best every day."[7] High agreement links to job satisfaction, effective performance, profitability, and customer loyalty. And the more strongly you agree with this statement, the more productive you are likely to be.

This brings us back to one core belief of AdverSelling: The best way to become more productive is different for every individual and every situation. That's why the only person who can find the answer is you. And it's why the process is structured to help you become more efficient in generating new sales tactics, and then testing them on the job to see what actually works.

Follow up

If I could tell you exactly what to do to increase sales, would you do it? I'm sure you'd *plan* to do it. But plans are often forgotten when the phone rings and a mini-crisis breaks out.

The best ideas in the world will not lead to sales unless you try them in the field. In the business best seller *Execution*, Larry Bossidy, Ram Charan, and Charles Burck argue that managers need to pay more attention to "the missing link between aspirations and results,"[8] the unglamorous discipline of getting things done.

Part of the power of AdverSelling comes from the fact that people are most likely to excel when they are given the freedom to follow up on their own ideas.

Psychologists have found that when people control their environment, they feel better and accomplish more.[9] For example, prisoners who are given control over small things in their environment such as TV sets and lights experience less stress and commit less vandalism. This type of finding has been replicated in a wide variety of environments, from nursing homes to homeless shelters. In addition, a review of forty-seven management studies[10] found that when workers make their own decisions, they are far more satisfied with their jobs.

In the best seller *The Tipping Point,* Malcolm Gladwell shows how relatively small events can have an enormous impact on mass trends, and quotes examples from sneaker fashions to Sesame Street to prove it (see Chapter 6). AdverSelling could help you find your personal tipping point, a technique that can take your sales to a new level.

The history of advertising is full of examples in which a single great idea changed an entire industry. Consider V&S Vin & Spirits, the company behind Absolut vodka. In 1979, Absolut was a tiny brand sold only in Sweden. Then they started an ad campaign that still runs today: artistic images of Absolut bottles, each with a short headline like Absolut Perfection and Absolut Magic. Today the company sells $600 million worth of vodka every year, and attributes much of its success to these ads (see Chapter 25).

Or consider De Beers, the diamond cartel that has controlled sales of over eighty percent of the world's rough diamonds for more than a century. They sell over $6 billion worth of diamonds every year, and experts trace much of their success to the "Diamonds are forever" ad campaign, which began in 1947. Indeed, the entire custom of diamond engagement rings can be traced to these ads (see Chapter 4).

Can AdverSelling help you achieve a breakthrough like Absolut or De Beers? You'll never know until you try.

AdverSelling's strength lies in its practical, down-to-earth empirical approach, and its philosophy that there is no one right way to sell. Different tactics work for different products, and even for different people selling the same product. AdverSelling fosters innovation, open-mindedness, and persistence, to energize your selling and help you define the tactics that work for you.

So why not start today? Identify a sales opportunity to focus on, turn to a chapter that sounds promising, and start finding new ways to increase your sales.

"She wrote me a John Deere letter. . .
something about me not listening enough, I don't know. . .
I wasn't really paying attention."
— Harry in the film Dumb and Dumber

Chapter 1

Attract attention

Advertisers will do almost anything to attract your attention. They have to, since you are bombarded with more than three thousand advertising messages every day.[11]

Consider the use of cute animals, like the Taco Bell Chihuahua. The tiny dog with the piercing eyes and lip-synched dialog appeared on TV often enough to become a pop culture icon in the 1990s. Why? Because his endless quest for the perfect taco helped Taco Bell to attract attention.

When you search Expedia or Travelocity to find a hotel online, the ones at the top of the list paid for that spot. Cereal companies pay extra to have their boxes displayed at eye level. To prevent you from skipping an ad by changing the channel during the Evening News, roadblock ads show the same commercial on all three networks at the same time. Roadblock ads have also been tried on the internet. On the day they launched the new F-150 truck in 2003, Ford Motor Company purchased banner ads on AOL, MSN and Yahoo for twenty-four hours.[12]

And then there's product placement, which creates product buzz and attracts attention without even placing a traditional ad. When the *Wall Street Journal* reviewed the most influential advertising of 2004,[13] their top picks

included Oprah Winfrey's giveaway of 276 new Pontiac
G6 cars – one for every member of the audience at her
season opening show. This was not an inexpensive
promotion: the cars would have cost about $7.5 million in
the showroom. But the giveaway generated more than
$100 million worth of publicity, including over seven
hundred TV stories in the week of the giveaway.

One reason that advertisers have to spend so much and
try so hard to attract attention is that we are all suffering
from information overload.

Two professors at the University of California at
Berkley[14] estimated that in 2002, enough new
information was created to fill thirty-seven thousand
digital libraries, each equal in size to the seventeen
million volumes at the Library of Congress.

Let's start with the world wide web. Have you seen that
commercial about the guy who "finished the internet?" If
he had actually visited every site on the web, it would
have taken eighty-one years.[15]

In 2003, Lyman and Varian called the world wide web the
"fastest growing new medium of all time," and calculated
its total information content at sixteen times the
information in the Library of Congress.

But wait, that's only the "surface web" of static, fixed web
pages. When you look up a book on Amazon, the
information you see on screen is not on a static page, it is
dynamically displayed from an underlying database
which has been called "the deep web." Then there's the
thirty-one billion emails sent every day, which over the
course of a year total more information than the surface
web and deep web combined. Then there are all those
instant messages. I'd give you the detailed totals, but
they are already out of date because their most recent
report summarized 2002, and annual new information is
growing by about thirty percent a year.

Sociologists and reporters have published an endless
supply of surveys showing how this information overload

interferes with productivity. In one survey, thirty-nine percent of a group of professionals reported that in a typical hour at work, they were interrupted at least six times.[16] In another,[17] one out of three managers reported that they "often feel overwhelmed at work," and half report that they work late or take work home as a result of trying to deal with too much information.

I could write an entire book full of statistics like this, but who's got time to read it? It's the twenty-first century. Your customers don't have time to buy, and you can barely find enough time to sell.

Francis Bacon wrote that knowledge is power. But that was in the seventeenth century, when books were scarce. Today, we are drowning in information, and new knowledge is likely to make you confused before it makes you powerful.

So if you want to attract customers' attention, be prepared to work at it.

Applying the principle

Over a century ago, sales experts devised the mnemonic AIDA to summarize four steps in selling to a customer: Attention, Interest, Desire, Action. Note what comes first: Attention.

Attracting attention is hardest when you are prospecting for new clients. In one recent survey,[18] two out of three sales people said prospecting is the activity they hate the most, about one out of three said they don't do it, and only three percent thought prospecting was productive.

Does that mean we can all stop cold calling? No, because eighty-eight percent of the companies in this same survey said that prospecting is absolutely essential to long term sales success, whether sales people like it or not.

This same survey analyzed how the best prospectors succeed in attracting attention, despite this challenging environment. Their approach is summarized in a four

stage model to improve prospecting called RIMS:
Research, Implication, Message Building, Sales Cycle.

The research stage involves more than just compiling a
list of people and phone numbers, and starts with a
hypothesis about who will be most interested in your
services, and why. What problems have you solved for
past customers? What other individuals or companies
face similar problems? What problems are most urgent
for your customers, and how could your product help?

Great prospectors create thought provoking messages.

The key is to figure out how you can provide value to
customers, even if buyers cannot verbalize the problem.
You need to help them see the problem in new ways, or
come up with unanticipated solutions.

The next stage is to think through the implications for
different audiences. Downward price pressure may have
one set of implications for sales managers who consider
discounts, and another set of implications for operations
people who need to cut costs.

This leads to the message building stage, in which great
prospectors craft a message tied to the implications. The
key at this stage is to provoke interest and attract
attention. You don't need to inform customers yet. At
this point you just need to hook their interest.

Now you may be thinking: That's easy to say and hard to
do. You're right. That's where the magic happens, when
you come up with an angle that attracts attention
without creating annoyance. That's why the first stage
consisted of research about your audience, and the second
stage was devoted to defining implications.

Nobody said it would be easy. But you need to figure out
a way to attract attention to the value of your product, or

you'll never get to the fourth stage – Sales Cycle – to get the prospect into your pipeline.

Reminders

- Show customers how you can add value (see Chapter 4).
- Focus on customer needs, not your credentials (see Chapter 5, Listen).
- Test your message over and over (see Chapter 6), constantly improving it until you succeed in provoking interest in your target audience.
- Come up with facts and figures to stimulate curiosity (see Chapter 9).
- Get referrals (see Chapter 10, Ask for help).
- If you have several target audiences, develop a different message for each (see Chapter 12, Personalize and customize).
- Improve your elevator speech (see Chapter 21, Less is more).
- Build relationships first, sell later (see Chapter 26, Don't stop).
- Analyze all your messages from a customer's point of view: If you were a customer, would this message attract your attention?
- Research your prospects' concerns, and build your message around their needs.
- Come up with a short and convincing answer to the question: "Why should I do business with you?"

Ask yourself

- If I were a prospect, would the sales message attract my attention?
- How could I change my initial message to provoke more interest?
- Should I spend more time developing and pre-testing my voice mail message before I start dialing?

*"If you can once engage people's pride, love, pity, ambition
(or whatever is their prevailing passion) on your side,
you need not fear what their reason can do against you."*
– Philip Dormer Stanhope

Chapter 2

Engage your customers

Have you ever won $10 million in the Publishers Clearinghouse Sweepstakes? Me either. But I'll bet you remember getting an envelope in the mail with the message: "You may already have won $10 million."[19] And maybe you've even ordered magazines from them, since about ten percent of the people who receive these mailings do buy.

Publishers Clearinghouse has become the world's largest independent magazine distributor by engaging their customers' interest. In the fifty years since, Harold and LuEsther Mertz started the company in their basement, Publishers Clearinghouse has awarded $187 million in sweepstakes prizes.[20]

If you did order a subscription, it is certainly possible that you started by deciding you wanted twelve months of *TV Guide* or *House Beautiful*, then shopped around until you found the best buy at Publishers Clearinghouse. But it seems far more likely that you are one of the many customers who thought that buying a magazine might increase your chances of winning, or who got pulled in by the "action devices" in the mailing.

Direct mail companies use the term "action devices" to describe anything that gets the customer interacting with a mailing, such as Yes and No stickers that must be moved around on the enclosed forms. Publishers

Clearinghouse mailings sometimes also require people to find hidden stickers, and to pick the prizes they may win. These action devices have been repeatedly shown to engage customer interest, and to "increase the pull" of a mailing, that is the number of people who respond. One minute you're moving stickers around, then the next thing you know you're ordering magazine subscriptions.

The need for tactics like this, or anything else which can engage customers' interest has never been higher. Jack Trout calls it the tyranny of choice: today's consumers simply have too many products to choose from. For some examples, see Table 2.[21]

TABLE 2		
THE EXPLOSION OF PRODUCT CHOICES		
Item	*Early 1970s*	*Late 1990s*
Varieties of pop tarts	3	29
Contact lens types	1	36
McDonald's menu items	13	43
Dental flosses	12	64
Types of Frito-Lay chips	10	78
Over the counter pain relievers	17	141
Running shoe styles	5	285
Airports	11,261	18,202
New book titles	40,530	77,446
Software titles	0	250,000

Source: Trout, J. Trout on strategy. USA: McGraw-Hill, 2004, p. 7.

Advertisers must find a way to cut through this clutter and engage consumers' interest. Trout's primary answer is to define your product's niche, as described in the book *Positioning: How to be seen and heard in the overcrowded marketplace* (see Chapter 17, Make a good first impression).[22]

Internet search ads engage customers by enabling advertisers to reach interested consumers at the very moment that they are looking. They can also be combined with other media. During the 2004 US Open, each time an ad was televised for Adidas's new R7 driver, traffic at the website jumped twenty-two percent. Golfers had their interest stimulated by the TV ad, and then went to the web to get detailed information, including videos showing how far your ball would go down the fairway, if only you used an R7.

The web offers many ways to engage customers and measure advertising effectiveness. New ads can be tested in hours; if nobody clicks, they can be discarded within a day.

A new technique called behavioral targeting also enables advertisers to track other websites visited and what they read at your website, and what ads they click on. All in a way that is designed to minimize privacy concerns by avoiding the collection of personal data about individual users.

Applying the principle

There was a time when companies thought that they could increase business by increasing customer satisfaction. But then a funny thing happened: Just about everybody figured out how to satisfy most of their customers, most of the time. Average levels of eighty percent are now common across all companies, and further improvements after eighty percent have been found to have limited impact on new business.[23]

The result is that in most industries, customer satisfaction is no longer a differentiator that will earn new business. These days, the bar is higher, and companies need to go beyond satisfaction to a deeper level of emotional connection or engagement. The Gallup organization has developed a brief questionnaire to measure the four major dimensions of engagement: confidence, integrity, pride, and passion. Here are the first few:[24]

> Company X is a name I can always trust.

> Company X always delivers on what it promises.

> Company X always treats me fairly.

> If a problem arises, I can always count on Company X to reach a fair and satisfactory resolution.

Notice that all four questions include the word "always," because engagement depends on consistency. They conclude that: "Since Gallup researchers have found that customer engagement leads to sustainable growth and enhanced profits, those sales reps and customer-facing employees who can generate customer engagement are worth their weight in gold."[25]

Reminders

- With prospects and new customers, find a way to engage interest immediately, even if you need to use a gimmick.
- Look for small actions which will draw people in.
- When you will give a presentation, pre-test it with colleagues, friends and family, and ask them to rate their level of interest.
- Watch your audience for signs of interest, or boredom.
- Keep your presentations fresh – change something every time you speak.
- With long-term customers, remember that the best path to more sales is to ensure a consistent experience that builds confidence and trust.
- Make customers aware of your pride in your work, and your passion for providing excellent service.

Ask yourself

- How can I engage the interest of new customers?
- What can I do to earn my customers' trust and loyalty?
- What can I do to inspire greater confidence?
- How would customers rate my integrity, pride, and passion?

"You talkin' to me?"
— Travis Bickle in the film Taxi Driver

Chapter 3

Appeal to self-interest

Burger King's "Have it your way" campaign in the 1970s is a great example of appealing to self-interest:

> Hold the pickles
> Hold the lettuce
> Special orders
> Don't upset us
> All we ask is
> That you let us
> Serve it your way

One TV spot followed "pickle-less Nicholas," a child who would not accept a hamburger with a pickle.[26] Now some parents would see this as a teaching opportunity. Life is hard, they might say, and sometimes you just have to learn to take the gherkin off your own bun. But Nicholas' parents must have been reading guides to permissive childrearing. They traveled from one fast food outlet to another, looking for a pickle-free burger. Which they found at Burger King. This campaign was so successful that Burger King has come back to the slogan several times.

Advertisers have a long history of appealing to self-interest. The self-improvement business got its start in the late nineteenth century with mail-in correspondence courses. By 1911, the University of Wisconsin correspondence program had several thousand students and even its own cheer:

> Pooh Pooh Harvard
> Pooh Pooh Yale
> I got my education
> Through the mail

Self-improvement ads run by the International Correspondence Schools nearly a century ago still ring true today: "More than ever before, money is what counts. The cost of living is mounting month by month....Somehow, you've simply got to increase your earnings." Their 1919 answer: mail order courses to improve your job prospects.

One famous ad showed a proud husband who had just completed ICS courses, and gotten a better job. He is handing money to his beaming wife, with the headline: "Here's an extra $50, Grace – I'm making real money now."[27]

For those whose self-esteem is based more on muscles than money, there's Charles Atlas,[28] originator of a famous comic strip ad entitled: "The insult that made a man out of Mac."

The story was based on an actual event in Atlas's life, when he was a ninety-seven pound weakling, at the beach in Coney Island with a girl prettier than he was.[29] When a muscle-bound lifeguard kicked sand in Atlas's face, the girlfriend said: "Oh don't let it bother you, little boy," and left with the other guy.

In the comic strip version of this life-altering moment, Mac is shown sometime later, saying: "Darn it. I'm sick and tired of being a scarecrow. I'll gamble a stamp and get Charles Atlas's free book." Which convinces him to pay what was then a small fortune (thirty dollars) for an eighty-page booklet describing the "dynamic tension exercise system," an early version of isometrics.

As the comic strip ad continues, Mac exercises for a few months, becomes muscle-bound, returns to the beach, and intimidates the bully. In the last panel, the same girlfriend of his dreams says: "Oh Mac, you ARE a real man after all."

The ads for Charles Atlas Ltd. became so well known that the phrase "ninety-seven pound weakling" made its way into the American vocabulary. At the beginning of the 1991 Gulf War, President George Bush (the first) described Saddam Hussein as "a classic bully who thinks he can kick sand in the face of the world."[30]

Advertisers often appeal to self-interest.

Perhaps the most extreme version of a self-interest commercial is "Daisy," a presidential election commercial that was shown only once[31] (but still made *Advertising Age's* list of the top one hundred commercials of the century).

Some background: It was 1964, less than a year since Kennedy had been assassinated and Vice President LBJ sworn in. Everyone remembered the 1962 Cuban Missile Crisis, and worried about the threat of nuclear war.

Johnson's 1964 opponent was the conservative Republican Barry Goldwater, who opposed the nuclear test ban treaty, and favored giving NATO field commanders authority to use tactical nuclear weapons without higher approval. According to one source, Goldwater had even said that it might make sense to "lob one into the men's room of the Kremlin."[32]

The commercial opened with a freckle-faced little girl standing in a field. She brushes back her hair as she counts daisy petals "three . . . four . . . five . . ." Then her voice is replaced by a technician's countdown, and a flash of light. The screen goes dark, an atomic mushroom cloud rises, and Johnson says: "These are the stakes. We must either learn to love each other or we must die.... Vote for President Johnson on November 3."

The Republicans screamed, and the commercial was never shown again. But Goldwater lost in a landslide, and the "Daisy" commercial is still cited as the beginning of negative advertising in modern political campaigns.

You will probably encounter resistance if you try the approach of the Daisy commercial: buy my product or die. But it's obvious that you are more likely to get cooperation and enthusiasm if you can show prospects "what's in it for me."

Psychological research suggests that it should be easy to relate material to self-interest, since "We tend to see ourselves as center stage . . . and we often see ourselves as responsible for events in which we played only a small role."[33]

In one study, research subjects remembered characters in a short story best when they had been asked to compare themselves to the character. In another, the information people remembered best was whatever had been said about them. If a test or horoscope flatters us, we believe it, and also are more likely to believe it comes from a valid source.[34]

This is related to another interesting fact about our self-image: most people consistently rate themselves as better than average. Ninety percent of managers rate their work performance above average, and most drivers say they are better than average, including those who have been hospitalized for accidents. Most people also say they are less prejudiced, more intelligent, and better looking than average. So in some ways, appealing to self-interest when you sell should not be too tough.

Applying the principle

Appealing to self-interest lies at the heart of every sale. But, like many things, it's not as easy as it sounds.

In *Solution Selling*, Michael T. Bosworth notes how important it is to "Diagnose before you prescribe."[35] Have you ever told prospects about the benefits of your product before you took the time to learn what they really want and need? Bosworth argues that sales people can build long term relationships only if they invest time at the start to understand each client's situation, perceptions and problems.

Solution selling distinguishes between three levels of self-interest, or need:

1. *Latent pain* implies that the buyer is not consciously aware that she needs your product. There are many possible reasons why the need may be latent. Maybe she's tried to solve the problem before, failed, and become convinced that there is no solution. Maybe the buyer just doesn't understand what your product can do. But whatever the reason, you'll never make a sale if the pain remains latent.

2. *Pain* implies that a buyer is consciously aware there's a problem, but does not see a solution, or feel an urgent need to find one. Bosworth says that sales people must work to get the buyer's attention and claim mindshare, so that she takes the time to focus on *your* problem. Only then can the buyer get to the next level.

3. *Vision of a solution* means that the buyer has an active idea of who will solve the problem, what they will do, when, and how.

This framework has led Bosworth to develop a number of sophisticated techniques for sales people to help buyers progress through the three levels. For example, he explains how to use "reference stories" in prospecting, to show how others in the same industry experienced pain, and what they did about it.[36] When solution selling is used effectively, it not only will help you to close the current sale, it will help you to build the foundation for the next one.

Another thing that can make self-interest tricky to assess is the fact that not all pains are created equal, especially in large sales with multiple buyers. Rick Page's *Hope Is Not a Strategy: The 6 Keys to Winning the Complex Sale* includes a diagram of different categories of needs which he calls the "Food Chain of Value" for a large organization.[37] It's also called the shark chart, because the needs at the bottom can be overwhelmed and eaten by the more important needs at the top. Starting near the bottom, they include:

- *Operational* benefits such as ease of use or sophisticated functionality. These are critical to the end-users of a product, but less important than many other things to upper management.

- *Cultural* benefits support the organization's value systems, and are more important than operational benefits to upper management.

- *Financial* benefits such as increased revenue and decreased costs are more important than operational and cultural matters, but typically less important than political or strategic factors.

- *Political* benefits, including the emotional impact for key executives, probably should not be more important than the factors listed above, but in the real world they often are.

- *Strategic* benefits directly address the issues that keep the CEO and other C-level executives awake at night. If your product is tied to a significant corporate initiative for market share or speed to market or anything else, and your competitor's product is not, you will win.

Reminders

- At the heart of every purchase, a buyer will select or reject your product based on a perception of personal benefits.
- Diagnose before you prescribe: take time to understand the buyer's perception of pain before you propose a solution.
- After you understand what a buyer needs, use language that links your benefits directly to their needs.
- In large company sales with multiple buyers, recognize that higher level needs such as strategic and political benefits may be more important than financial and operational benefits.
- Be specific.
- Eliminate anything that would make you a risky choice, and try to combine the smallest personal risk with the greatest personal payoff.
- Help others get what they want.
- Determine, and speak to, how the client wants to feel after the purchase is made.
- Since a single product may have many different benefits to different people, it is important to understand exactly what each client wants and needs.
- Develop case studies and client examples that demonstrate benefits to people who are in the same industry as your prospects.
- Remember that "Telling isn't selling," and avoid focusing on features instead of benefits.

Ask yourself

- What do my clients want and need?
- How does my product meet those needs?
- How can I ensure that prospects understand the benefits of my product?
- If several people are involved in a decision, how can I insure that each gets what they want and need?

"The whole value of the dime
is knowing what to do with it."
— Ralph Waldo Emerson

Chapter 4

Add value

You could argue that almost every ad in history has attempted to communicate the product's value. But some ads go so far beyond communication that they add and enhance value.

According to the *Business Week* brands survey quoted in Chapter 15, Intel is the fifth most valuable brand in the world, with a value over $30 billion. Intel is the company that invented the microprocessor in 1971, to serve as the brains inside your PC. When the "Intel Inside" campaign began in 1991, few people had ever heard of microprocessors, much less cared what brand they owned. But Intel was losing market share to cheaper competitors and needed to do something dramatic to protect their position at the top of the market.

They decided on a radical approach: sell directly to PC end-users. Until that time, all ads had been aimed at technical decision makers and their bosses, in publications like *PC Magazine* and the *Wall Street Journal*. The idea of trying to sell microprocessors to end-users struck some experts as laughable. As one wrote in the *LA Times*: "It's money down the drain . . . The public is . . . too unsophisticated to listen."[38]

But Intel went ahead and ran "Intel Inside" ads in *Architectural Digest, National Geographic, Working Woman, Parenting*, and *Bon Appetit*. The campaign started in the early 90s, when home PCs were starting to make their way into every den and home office. Sales of Intel chips increased sixty-three percent in the first year of the campaign, and have continued to climb ever since.[39] All because they were able to enhance value by convincing you to care about what chip is inside your PC.

An even better example of enhancing value comes from the story of diamonds and the role played by De Beers Consolidated Mines. The company was founded in 1888 by Cecil Rhodes, a few decades after diamonds were discovered in Kimberley, South Africa. At that time, South Africa was overrun by independent miners. Rhodes secured $5 million in financial backing from the Rothschild family, and bought out all the claims so that he could control the worldwide supply of this precious stone. Which the company did, quite successfully. De Beers controlled over eighty percent of the diamond market for most of the twentieth century, and strictly limited the number of diamonds that came on the market.[40]

After the supply of diamonds was strictly controlled, to maximize profits all they needed was more demand. Traditionally, diamonds were bought only by the rich, and there were not enough rich people in the world to meet De Beers' growth projections. The 1930s Depression did not help one bit, when diamond sales dropped fifty percent.

Around this time, Harry Oppenheimer, heir to the De Beers fortune, hired the N.W. Ayer advertising agency to create a campaign built around the notion that when a young woman gets engaged, she absolutely must have a diamond ring, and no other jewel will do.[41]

There was a brief timeout for World War II, when the company's emphasis shifted to military uses of industrial diamonds. But in 1947, copy writer Frances Garety invented a tag line that is still used in diamond ads today: "Diamonds are Forever."[42]

These advertisements were combined with a massive public relations campaign. A confidential internal De Beers memo[43] described one 1950s campaign in which speakers gave educational talks to high school assemblies about the history of diamonds: "All of these lectures revolve around the diamond engagement ring, and are reaching thousands of girls in their assemblies, classes and informal meetings in our leading educational institutions." Other N.W. Ayer employees worked on Hollywood, and quoted such successes as Marilyn Monroe singing "Diamonds are a girl's best friend" in the 1953 film *Gentlemen Prefer Blondes.*

Some ads have been enormously successful by enhancing value.

In 1950, about half of all young US couples bought engagement rings. Ten years later, the proportion had increased to eighty percent. A comparable campaign was started in Japan, which had no tradition of diamond rings. There, the percent of couples with diamond engagement rings rose from six percent in 1967 to about sixty-seven percent by the early 1980s.[44]

The "Diamonds are forever" slogan has survived several attempts at updates. De Beers attempted to appeal to the self-gratification trend of the 1970s by re-casting the slogan as: "Diamonds are for now." But this was soon dropped, and the original phrase was restored: "Diamonds are forever."[45]

These campaigns have been so successful that some young women seem to measure the sincerity of potential spouses by the percent of income they are willing to send to the local jeweler. The ads provide a handy guideline for the men: if you truly love your partner, you will spend about two months of your gross income. In exchange, the young couple will get a small stone that has been picked out of a hill in South Africa for a few dollars. Now that's what I call enhanced value.

The add value approach was perfected by Rosser Reeves, Bates' creative director in the fifties and sixties, and David Ogilvy's rival and brother-in-law. Reeves became known as the "prince of hard sell" for his concept of cutting through the clutter of competing messages with a Unique Selling Proposition (USP). He argued that every ad should focus on a single rational message which described unique products benefits, over and over. Reeves believed this approach could be applied even when uniqueness had to be manufactured. "The claims may be true for all brands, not just our own," admitted Reeves.[46] "But we tell people about them."

Reeves was also a strong believer in research, and invented techniques to test his campaigns, year after year. He heaped scorn on creative approaches to advertising, and measured success strictly by "usage pull," a figure he invented to measure the number of people who remembered the ads, and the proportion who actually bought the product.

Reeves believed that once you found a Unique Selling Proposition that worked, you should stick with it, until research showed that it had stopped working. That's one reason why his most famous campaign – for Anacin – went on so long (see Chapter 16, Repeat the message).

Many of Reeves' Unique Selling Propositions were repeated so often that they still seem familiar today. If it were not for Rosser Reeves, none of us would know that Colgate cleans your breath while it cleans your teeth, that Wonder Bread helps build strong bodies twelve ways, and that M&Ms melt in your mouth, not in your hands.

Applying the principle

According to Neil Rackham in the classic *SPIN Selling*: "The building of perceived value is probably the single most important selling skill in larger sales."[47] The anagram SPIN refers to four critical categories of questions: Situation, Problem, Implication, Need-Payoff.

Most sales people are naturally good at the first two categories – situation and problem questions – but need to learn to use the second two – implication and need-payoff questions.

Situation questions are for fact finding. For example, if you were selling a software product that tracks client information, you might ask: "How do you currently keep track of prospects' names and addresses?" or "How many years have you been using this system?"

Problem questions get at the pain that prospects feel, their dissatisfactions and difficulties, such as "Are you happy with the tracking system you're using now?" and "What are some of the biggest problems with your current system?"

Implication questions take the dialog one step further, by focusing on implications and consequences. Implication questions probe beneath the surface of problems, to localize the pain. Suppose that when a prospect was asked about problems with the current sales database, she replied that she sometimes observed problems synchronizing data from the entire team's laptops.

One implication question would be: "Does that mean that managers do not always have the latest data from the entire team?" Another would ask: "Are people wasting time trying to synchronize?" In studies of over 35,000 sales calls, Rackham found that implication questions are strongly linked to success in large sales.

Need-payoff questions dig the deepest by explicitly discussing the value of your solution, as in "Why would it be useful for managers to have up to the minute data from every sales person?" or "Why would it be useful to reduce the time spent on synchronization?" This is the most subtle category, the one least likely to be used by

[handwritten margin notes:]
- where do most customers come from?
- are you happy w/ your cust. base
- 1. of new customers
- wht are some of your challenges getting customers
- what type of ads work?
- why would it be useful to

new sales people, and it is closely linked with success in large sales.

In an age of information overload, the ability to add perceived value may be the single most important way for sales people to stand out in a crowded marketplace.

In the book *Stop Selling, Start Partnering*, Larry Wilson takes this idea further with a checklist for building a true partnership,[48] based on five elements:

1. *The wonderful paradox*, according to Wilson, is that when you genuinely put your customer's interest first, it will ultimately be to your benefit, even though this may seem naïve or altruistic on the surface.

2. *Break it, shake it, and remake it.* The mindset of partnering is that everything can and should be improved. Everyone in the selling organization should constantly ask "What can we do better?" and then proceed to do it.

3. *Manage the moments of truth.* Each time your customer deals with your organization, whether calling for you to solve a problem or begin a new order, is a "moment of truth," and companies that are committed to partnering must manage these interactions to insure that clients are fully satisfied.

4. *Value-added service* implies not only meeting customer expectations, but constantly exceeding them.

5. *Run toward problems* since problems are inevitable in any relationship, and the success of a partnership involves solving them quickly, honestly, and creatively.

Reminders

- Become more than a supplier to your customer, become a partner.
- Build trust, which will allow you to explore opportunities to help.
- When working with new customers, focus on the unique features which are most valuable to them.
- Become perceived as an expert – not just on what you sell, but on industry trends that your clients care about.
- Use *implication questions* to probe beneath the surface of the pain that clients feel.
- Use *need-payoff questions* to make clients explicitly aware of the benefits of your solution.

Ask yourself

- Do I genuinely understand what keeps my clients up at night?
- How can I help?
- What can I do to foster a partner mentality?
- Do prospects believe that I can add value for them?
- Could I improve my questioning techniques to help clients perceive the implications of their problems, and the need-payoff of my solution?

"Remember that silence is sometimes the best answer."
– Dalai Lama

Chapter 5

Listen

In the 1980s, a famous series of ads showed groups of prosperous people at noisy restaurants, parties, and meetings. In each ad, one affluent person would lean over and say to another, "My broker is E.F. Hutton, and E.F. Hutton says . . ." When the crowd fell silent, the tag line would appear: "When E.F. Hutton talks, people listen."

Maybe it's just a coincidence that E.F. Hutton disappeared soon after these ads were shown. In December 1987, Shearson Lehman acquired the eighty-three year old brokerage at fire sale prices, after problems ranging from management fights for control to bad publicity and allegations of check kiting and embezzlement.

But I believe that the ads were a sign of the arrogance that helped lead to the company's downfall. E.F. Hutton should have been listening to its customers, not the other way around. As the cliché goes, that's why you have two ears, and one mouth.

In *The Seven Habits of Highly Effective People*, Stephen Covey says: "If I were to summarize the single most important principle in the field of interpersonal relationships, listening is the key."[49]

In the book *Primal Leadership*, Daniel Goleman, Richard Boyatzis and Annie McKee argue that listening skills are also vital for leadership.[50] An effective leader must be able to sense how employees feel, and then channel that energy into the most productive directions.

The skill of listening can even help you get a job. When business leaders were asked to rate the most important characteristics they look for in hiring people, seventy-three percent rated listening as an "extremely important" skill.[51] But when the same group was asked how many high school graduates have good listening skills, the answer was nineteen percent.

If you want to become a better listener, there are dozens of books to read, and even a professional academic organization you can join (the International Learning Association, www.listen.org). Meanwhile, these eight steps can get you started:

1. Keep people talking. Paraphrase, summarize, and restate what you hear. When you agree with people, they will think that you are smart. Especially if you don't interrupt them or argue.
2. Be prepared with good questions. The ones listed below in Reminders will help you get started.
3. Don't get distracted. If you turn to watch someone walking by, people may think you are not completely aware of how interesting they are.
4. Take notes. Writing down what people say shows that what they say is important, and that you are paying attention. Just put the pen down if the talk turns to the confidential.
5. Respond to the speaker's nonverbal cues including eye contact, smiling, and frowning.
6. Watch your own nonverbal cues. When you are listening to a customer, maintain steady eye contact, lean forward, smile and nod to communicate how fascinating they are.
7. Establish genuine interest by asking questions that you care about.
8. Keep quiet. Only one person should speak at a time. When you're listening, that's not you.

Applying the principle

It can take you weeks or months to get an appointment. So what do you do when you finally get there? How much do you talk, and how much do you listen? Which do you think the customer will be more interested in: talking about himself, or listening about you? Experts differ on whether you should listen fifty percent of the time or seventy percent or some other number.[52] But all agree you should listen a lot.

According to sales guru Brian Tracy: "Active sincere listening leads to easier sales, higher earnings, and greater enjoyment from the sales profession."[53] Tracy lists four main benefits:

1. Listening builds trust. Tracy cites an annual survey from the Purchasing Manager's Association of America, stating that the single biggest complaint of professional purchasers is that sales people talk too much. If you show that you are interested in understanding what people really need, they are more likely to trust that you can provide it.
2. Listening lowers resistance. It helps to make customers feel relaxed and comfortable instead of tense and defensive.
3. Listening builds self-esteem. Everyone wants to be listened to. So when a sales person listens, it reinforces the idea that the customer's views are important, and helps them to feel better about themselves.
4. Listening builds character and self-discipline. Some people are not too exciting. When you listen to one, it's easy to start daydreaming about whether you should have lunch at Panera's or Mickey D's. But the more boring your customer is, the more character you will build by listening. And the better you understand what they want, the more likely you are to close a sale.

If you think you could improve in this area, start with Kevin Daley's book *Socratic Selling: How to Ask the Questions that Get the Sale*.[54] The book analyzes several categories of probing questions, including the ones listed below.

Reminders

- When you talk to customers, remember that the customer is more interesting than you.
- Master the art of asking questions that are easy to answer.
- Use draw probes, such as:
  - Tell me more about ____.
  - Give me an example of ____.
  - What else should I know about ____?
- Use access probes, such as
  - How does ____ fit the picture?
  - Talk to me about your experience with ____.
  - How do you handle ____?
- Ask easily answered questions about urgency, such as:
  - What makes this urgent?
  - Why is this important right now?
- Ask easily answered questions about irritants, such as
  - What bothers you most?
  - How tough a position does this put you in?
- Ask easily answered questions about motivators, such as:
  - How does this affect you?
  - Why is this important to you?
- Ask easily answered questions to elicit decisions, such as "If you were to go ahead with ____ when would you ____?"
- Get approval and agreement with easily answered questions, such as:
  - How does that sound?
  - Do I have it right?

- Keep thinking "who, what, when, where, why, and how," and you can probe for hours.
- And remember that the key to effective listening is genuine interest. If that doesn't work, ask yourself what's getting in the way?

Ask yourself

- In my last few meetings with customers, did I listen at least fifty percent of the time?
- Could I get a better understanding of my customers' needs if I spent less time talking and more time listening?
- Would people to tell me more if I practiced becoming a better listener?

> *"Test everything, retain what is good."*
> *– 1 Thessalonians 5:21*

Chapter 6

Test early and often

If you rely strictly on your own opinion, and fail to test your ideas, you could end up like Dick Rowe. Never heard of him? That's because he ignored the power of testing.

In 1962, when Dick Rowe headed Decca Record's London office, he was approached by Brian Epstein, manager of a new group called the Beatles. "They will be bigger than the Shadows," Epstein promised. But Rowe refused to cut a record, saying: "Groups are out . . . .The boys won't go, Mr. Epstein . . . .We know these things."[55]

The advertising industry has a deep commitment to testing to avoid mistakes based on personal bias. Ad campaigns are often tested and refined through weeks or months of surveys, focus groups, and sales tests.[56]

As early as the 1880s, the Phoenix Home Life Mutual Insurance Companies compared the response to different versions of an ad, and tracked which ads produced the biggest response. In a typical test, two identical ads were run with different headlines, and the responses were sent to two different post office boxes. The ad agency provided regular reports of where and when each ad appeared, what they had cost, how many leads and sales they had produced, the cost per lead, and the cost per sale.[57] Over time, they gradually discovered some basic rules for headlines (see Chapter 20).

Chain restaurants constantly test new foods. If you're trying to lose weight, McDonald's sees you as part of the ever expanding market for low-fat, low-calorie, and low-carbohydrate fast food. Their chefs are working overtime testing products to improve their bottom line, and yours, like the Go Active salad pack, complete with a list of exercises and a pedometer.

From a nutritionist's standpoint, the problem with McDonald's tests is that they keep leading to the same conclusion: many consumers don't want healthy food. What they want is more along the lines of McGriddles, the company's most successful new product in years: pancakes with sausage, bacon, eggs and/or cheese conveniently baked right in, along with "the taste of maple syrup."

As McGriddle's heavily tested ads put it: "Weird. But a good kind of weird" and "Bizarre, but yummy." Health food proponents may not like the conclusions of McDonald's market testing, but there is no doubt that testing the products and the ads can be the difference between a successful fast food, and Spam musubi (a breakfast tested at McDonald's in Hawaii—cooked Spam served sushi-style on a block of rice, wrapped in seaweed).

In *The Tipping Point*, Malcolm Gladwell describes three key elements behind social trends: focus, test, and believe. "Those who are successful in creating social epidemics do not just do what they think is right. They test their intuitions."[58]

He cites the example of social science researchers who made *Sesame Street* a success by inventing a new testing device called "The Distracter." A slide show of attention-grabbing images was set up next to a TV showing *Sesame Street*. Research assistants recorded whether preschoolers were looking at the TV or the slides each time the slide changed, every 7.5 seconds. Then the writers changed each *Sesame Street* episode until it held attention at least eighty-five percent of the time.

When "The Distracter" was used to test the first five pilot episodes in 1969, the researchers were surprised to learn that some of the elements their experts loved best were ignored by pre-schoolers. Cute animal shots bombed. A punning character called the Man from Alphabet failed so badly that he never made it to the air. And segments that lasted more than three or four minutes lost attention.

Ad testing techniques have been refined for over a century.

The biggest surprise involved the characters on *Sesame Street* itself. Child psychology experts had convinced the writers that it was important to avoid mixing fantasy with reality. When the first five episodes were shot on a test basis, the Muppet characters were isolated in all puppet mini-episodes, while the characters on *Sesame Street* itself were all real adults and children.

When they tested these episodes with "The Distracter," researchers learned that pre-school viewers were riveted to the Muppets, and turned away during the all-human segments.

As a result, before the first show went on the air, they reshot the pilot episodes, and invented Big Bird, Oscar the Grouch and Snuffleupagus to live on Sesame Street.[59]

Without testing, *Sesame Street* might have been just another high-minded and high-priced failure that fit the preconceptions of experts, and missed its audience. With testing, it became one of the most influential programs in the history of television.

Which is not to say that testing is an exact science, nor that it works every time. Success cannot be guaranteed by data. You are also going to need some shrewdness in analyzing results, and a little bit of luck. But if you test early and often, it will substantially increase your chances of success.

Applying the principle

There are no simple truths in sales, and the only way to find out what works for you is to test and improve. That's why the most successful sales people have a deep seated practical streak, and are always ready to try something new as soon as the old tactics stop working.

Testing can challenge experts' most treasured beliefs. Consider the difference between open and closed questions. Open questions encourage customers to talk, with phrases like "Tell me about your experience with _____," or "How do you think _____ could be improved?" Closed questions elicit short answers, often yes or no, such as "Could you buy our product within this year's budget?" or "How many people report to you?"

You may have been told that open questions are more effective in sales, because it is a good thing to get people talking. However, when Neil Rackham tested this idea by observing actual sales meetings, he found that it was simply not true: "There was no identifiable relationship between success and the use of open or closed questions."[60] For example, in one study of the top producers at a high tech company, some used all open ended questions, some used all closed questions, and some used a mixture of the two. The content of the question mattered a great deal, but its form did not matter at all.

Rackham has published some of the most sophisticated studies of selling, and did not jump to the conclusion that his finding applied in every sales situation. His studies focused on large sales for high revenue products, and it is possible that open and closed questions work differently for smaller sales.

Which brings us to the heart of the matter: tactics that work in one situation or one industry may fail in another.

Indeed, tactics that work for other top producers on your team may not work for you, if you have different personal styles and different selling strengths. That's why selling is an art rather than a science, and why generic approaches to sales are of limited value to experienced professionals.

Reminders

- Try different sales tactics, and track the results.
- Be open to the fact that systematic data from a large group may challenge some of your beliefs.
- For example, if you are writing letters to get a meeting, try sending out two different versions, then track the groups to see how many meetings you got with each.
- Pre-test every important sales communication. This can be as elaborate as videotaping a practice session for a big presentation, or as simple as asking a colleague to react to your next important email or voice mail message.
- Test your elevator speech over and over (see Chapter 21). Try it out on a friend, then ten minutes later, ask him to repeat your message. You may be appalled at how little people remember. Keep changing the message until people remember your main point.
- When practical, test typical audience members. In our research, we've found a huge gap between the way audience members respond, and the way experts think they will respond.[61] So the closer you can get to your audience, the more accurate your results will be.
- On the other hand, sales is not a science experiment,[62] and an imperfect test is better than no test at all. If it's not practical to test typical audience members, test a co-worker, a family member, or your sales associate at Brooks Brothers.
- If you're designing a mass campaign, you may be tempted to design an elaborate market test. But researchers have found that several small tests yield

more information than one large test.[63]   So if you can
afford ten testers, don't use them all at once. Test
your first draft on three people, your second draft on
three more, and your third draft on the final four.

Ask yourself

- Should I compare several approaches to prospecting,
  and track the results?
- Do I need help to pre-check letters and emails?
- Should I videotape a rehearsal for my next sales
  presentation?
- Should I ask a few friends to react to my voice mail
  message?
- How should I practice my elevator speech?

"Whenever you are asked if you can do a job,
tell 'em, 'Certainly I can!'
Then get busy and find out how to do it."
— Teddy Roosevelt

Chapter 7

Be optimistic and credible

In a perfectly logical world, the content of a message would be more important than the way it is presented. But if you live on the planet Earth, the style of your presentation often matters more than its content, starting with your optimism and credibility.

When advertisers talk about product benefits, they optimistically accentuate the positive and eliminate the negative. You've probably seen ads promising that a particular soap will make you smell as fresh as the great outdoors. But you've never seen one that says, "If you *don't* use this soap, you will smell like a chicken accidentally left thawing on the counter before you went on vacation for a month."

That's because advertisers have learned the hard way that positive messages sell, and negative messages do not. Gillette once launched a massive ad campaign for a shampoo with the name "For Oily Hair Only" in large letters on the bottle.[64] It flopped. It is one thing to buy a shampoo that mentions oily hair in fine print at the bottom. It is quite another to pick up a brand that shouts your problem to everyone who walks by your shopping cart.

Psychologists have found that optimism is fairly consistent throughout life. One study interviewed the Harvard graduating class in 1946, and then interviewed them again more than three decades later.[65] The 1946 optimists were not only still optimistic in 1980, they were also healthier. That link between optimism and health has been repeatedly seen in studies ranging from colds and the flu to survival rates for breast cancer.[66]

Positive messages sell, negative messages do not.

Self-confidence is good for you too. People with high self-esteem are less neurotic, less likely to be addicted to alcohol and drugs, and less likely to suffer from stress-related disorders such as ulcers and insomnia. In fact, they are just plain happier.[67]

If you lack self-confidence, fake it. It works. Have you heard that visualizing success will help you actually become more successful? That works too.

Studies of court cases have found that both experts and eyewitnesses are more likely to be believed when they appear self-assured and confident. In experimental studies, persuasion follows from nonverbal cues of self-confidence, including a low rate of speech errors, a steady body posture, and an authoritative tone of voice.[68] In another study, videotaped witnesses were judged as more believable if they looked the questioner right in the eye instead of gazing downward.[69]

And if your self-confidence needs a little boost, start with some "self-selling." According to the song in *Bye Bye Birdie,* when you need to cheer up, just "put on a happy face." It works. Psychologist James Laird monitored electrical activity in facial muscles, and told college students to smile. When the smiling muscles were activated, the students rated cartoons as funnier, and also felt happier. And when they were told to "pull your brows together" they felt angry.

If you doubt this, the next time you feel a little depressed, stand in front of a mirror and force yourself into a big, dopey grin. If that doesn't make you a little happy, email your psychiatrist.

Self-selling goes far beyond dopey grins. In another experiment people were instructed to imagine themselves being hardworking and successful on a challenging task. They did well. Others were told to imagine themselves failing, and fail they did.[70]

Repeating a statement out loud can also be helpful. There's no better way to feel involved than to say you're involved. Again, this can work even if you start out just mouthing the words.

Self-confidence can go a long way, but at the end of the day the audience has to agree that you are credible and worthy of being believed. Over two thousand years ago, Aristotle wrote in *Rhetoric*: "We believe good men more fully and more readily than others: this is generally true whatever the question is, and absolutely true where exact certainty is impossible and opinions are divided."[71]

Advertisers often take advantage of this fact by recruiting credible pitchmen. When Tiger Woods tells you which driver to buy, you will listen.

The endorser does not need to be a celebrity. Do you remember the Subway sandwich campaign featuring Jared, the guy who lost hundreds of pounds by incorporating Subway low-fat sandwiches into his diet? The ads showed Jared before and after, and his brush with fame must have stretched to at least sixteen or seventeen minutes.

In 1951, Carl Hovland and Walter Weiss performed one of the first and most famous tests of credibility and persuasion. The experiment was performed before atomic-powered submarines had been invented, and the question was whether they would be built in the next few years.

Two groups of people read the same argument. Half were told it came from a credible source – physicist J. Robert Oppenheimer – and the other half were told that it came from an unreliable source of propaganda—*Pravda*, the official newspaper of Soviet Communism. People's opinions were measured before and after reading the argument. Those who thought the argument came from Oppenheimer changed their view; those who thought the same ideas came from *Pravda* were not influenced.[72]

In the end, the single most important thing you can do to increase both credibility and self-confidence is to do your homework. As Mark Twain put it: "It takes me at least three weeks to prepare an impromptu speech."

Applying the principle

For as long as professionals have been selling, their managers have recognized the importance of positive thinking. When Ulysses S. Grant published his memoirs in 1885, canvassers sold the book door to door. Ten thousand sales people were given a thirty-seven page manual entitled "How to Introduce the Personal Memoirs of U. S. Grant." The section on "How to Leave the House" described the optimism they were expected to show even after losing a sale: "Shower smiles on the people as bountifully as though you had received an order for ten copies – then walk off treading the ground as though victory sat enthroned upon your brow."[73]

This optimism paid off: Grant's memoirs sold 325,000 copies in the first year, and his family ultimately received almost $450,000 in royalties, the equivalent of $8 million today.[74]

Optimism has been proven equally important in modern sales. In the 1980s, Metropolitan Life Insurance commissioned studies of the five thousand new agents they hired every year. Half quit in their first twelve months, and eighty percent left within four years.[75] The annual cost of this unsuccessful hiring was seventy-five million dollars per year to Metropolitan Life, and much higher to all the sales people who wasted several years of their life.

The most successful agents were optimists.

Now it's very hard to sell life insurance. For both successful and unsuccessful agents, most sales calls fail. That's why it's called a numbers game – you have to be willing to approach a very large number of people for your low success rate to produce a good living.

To the researchers' surprise, they found that in the first year the percentage of success was quite similar for agents who lasted four years, and those who quit. What was different was the way they interpreted their many failures. The most successful sales agents were consistently optimistic. When they lost a sale, they never said it was because "selling life insurance is hard" or "I'm no good at it." Instead, every unsuccessful sale was an exception: "that guy was too busy" or "they just happened to be eating when I called." The sales people that lasted were always convinced that success was just around the corner. And so it was.

Psychologist Martin Seligman developed a psychological test of optimism – called the Attributional Style Questionnaire – and compared test scores to performance at Metropolitan Life over several years. In one study, the sales people who scored in the top ten percent in optimism sold eighty-eight percent more insurance than the bottom ten percent. In another, sales people whose optimism scores were in the bottom half were twice as likely to quit as those in the top half.

Seligman later reported that life insurance agents were the most optimistic group they ever studied, more optimistic than car salesmen, West Point plebes, presidential candidates, and star athletes in swimming and baseball.

Sales managers have long worked to instill optimism in their teams. As the President of National Cash Register around 1900, John Patterson taught his sales people to "take it for granted that everyone can buy,"[76] and consistently referred to every prospect as a "probable purchaser."

To prove that anything was possible if only you believed, Patterson once organized a team of workmen to make an office building disappear overnight during a company convention. While the sales people slept, the workmen knocked down a large office building and replaced it with a patch of grass.[77] The point was remembered.

This is not to say that optimism is an advantage in every profession. If you were flying to Europe, would you want the FAA inspector who certified the safety of your aircraft to be an optimist? When you get tax advice from your CPA, do you want an optimist who believes there's no chance the IRS will ever audit you?

But in the sales profession, optimism is clearly an advantage. So if you are a pessimistic sales professional, and you don't want to switch to another career, you should consider working on this by actively changing the way you react to adversity and setbacks. Detailed suggestions can be found in psychologist Martin Seligman's book *Learned Optimism*.[78]

Reminders

- Accentuate the positive and eliminate the negative, because positive messages sell and negative messages do not.
- Start by assuming that prospects will buy from you. The only question is when.
- Maintain enthusiasm by repeating positive affirmations to yourself, such as: I will close this sale because I have the best product.
- Invite customers to imagine how their lives will be improved after they buy your product.

- Be optimistic about the close.
- When dealing with pessimistic buyers, remain upbeat and always return the discussion to the positive side.
- With tough customers, at some point you may want to just go for the close, no matter how low the chances of success. What have you got to lose?
- In addition to optimism, build credibility by learning and studying until you truly become an expert.
- Always tell the truth – even when it hurts.
- Don't raise expectations you cannot meet.
- Have a firm grip on the true benefits of your product.
- Prove your credibility by leveraging your network of satisfied customers. If you are selling to a new CPA, encourage her to call other CPAs you've worked with in the past.
- In the end, remember that enthusiasm matters more than knowledge.

Ask yourself

- Do customers perceive me as optimistic and credible?
- Do I always remain positive and upbeat?
- Do I project energy and confidence?
- Do I give non-verbal cues that I strongly believe what I am saying?
- What could I do to become even more positive?
- Could I increase my credibility by learning more about my customers' industry?
- Do I belong to the right professional associations?
- Am I doing enough reading, writing and study to maintain my credibility?

"Creativity is allowing yourself to make mistakes.
Art is knowing which ones to keep."
— Scott Adams

Chapter 8

Be creative

When *Advertising Age* rated the top one hundred
campaigns of the twentieth century,[79] the ad ranked
number one was chosen for its creativity: Volkswagen's
1959 "Think Small" campaign. The ads were developed
by Doyle Dane Bernbach, the agency that helped launch
the "golden age of advertising."

The Volkswagen certainly faced some of the biggest
public relations obstacles of the century. The car had
originally been designed by Ferdinand Porsche in 1937,
as a pet project of Adolph Hitler.[80] The VW ad campaign
was launched when World War II memories were fresh,
just fourteen years after the fall of Berlin.

The Volkswagen brand had been rebuilt after the war
around a high quality, low cost "people's car" that the
masses could depend on. At that time, the American auto
industry was dominated by the big three: General
Motors, Ford, and Chrysler. In 1950, Americans
purchased six million cars built in Detroit, and 330
Volkswagens.

Automobile ads stressed fantasy and competed to offer
the largest, most luxurious dream model. The Doyle
Dane Bernbach ads offered a creative alternative
approach. Extravagant and often vague claims were
replaced by simple straightforward statements of fact,
with a touch of self-deprecating humor.

TABLE 3

TOP 10 ADVERTISING CAMPAIGNS
OF THE 20TH CENTURY

---

1. Volkswagen, "Think Small", 1959
2. Coca-Cola, "The pause that refreshes", 1929
3. Marlboro, The Marlboro Man, 1955
4. Nike, "Just do it", 1988
5. McDonald's, "You deserve a break today", 1971
6. De Beers, "A diamond is forever", 1948
7. Absolut Vodka, The Absolut Bottle, 1981
8. Miller Lite beer, "Tastes great, less filling", 1974
9. Clairol, "Does she . . . or doesn't she?", 1957
10. Avis, "We try harder", 1963

Source: Garfield, Bob. "Top 100 Advertising
Campaigns of the Century." *Advertising Age.*
www.adage.com/century/campaigns.html

At a time when car makers added bigger tail fins every year and advertisers shot photos to make big cars look even bigger, the VW ads were low key, with over two-thirds empty white space. In one of the most famous, the upper left corner has only a small photo of a VW Beetle. At the bottom, the headline "Think Small" is followed by a few lines of text, including: "Some people who drive our little flivver don't even think thirty-two miles to the gallon is going any great guns....Or never needing anti-freeze. Or racking up forty thousand miles on a set of tires."[81]

Another ad in this campaign combined a VW photo with a one word headline: "Lemon." The text explained, "This Volkswagen missed the boat. The chrome strip on the glove compartment is blemished and must be replaced.

Chances are you wouldn't have noticed it; Inspector Kurt Kroner did."[82]

This "honesty campaign" appealed to the antiestablishment crowd, and essentially created the American trend toward compact cars. VW sales increased by about fifty percent in the first year after the ads appeared, and continued to rise to a peak of 569,696 cars in 1970.[83]

Another car campaign famous for its creativity was David Ogilvy's 1957 campaign for Rolls Royce. These long print ads described thirteen specific and concrete reasons why you should buy the luxurious Rolls Royce Silver Cloud, then priced at the 1950s incredibly high price of $13,995. The headline highlighted the first of thirteen facts: "At sixty miles an hour, the loudest noise in this new Rolls Royce comes from the electric clock."[84] The rest of the ad provided detail for all thirteen points, including: "The engineers use a stethoscope to listen for axle-whine," "The coach work is given five coats of primer paint, and hand-rubbed between each coat, before nine coats of finishing paint go on," and "You can get such optional extras as an Espresso coffee-making machine . . . a bed [and] . . . hot and cold water for washing."[85]

Ogilvy believed that some types of advertising creativity led to flashy ads with little substance. His agency used their creativity to build on a solid foundation of facts, because he believed, "The customer is not a moron, she is your wife."[86]

Applying the principle

I could say "be creative" when you sell. But that's a little like advising "be smart." It's easy to say, but hard to do.

Fortunately, advertising agencies and others have developed a number of systematic techniques to foster creative thinking. For example, in the book *Creative Advertising*,[87] Mario Pricken offers fifteen "rules of creative teamwork," including:

- Go into meetings with a clear goal.
- Avoid idea killers.
- Grab ideas and run with them.
- Look for the positive in other people's ideas.
- Make mistakes and have fun doing it.
- Wait before evaluating ideas.
- Stick with it, the best ideas are yet to come.

Creative Advertising includes a "KickStart" catalog of two hundred questions to stimulate creativity in meetings. Many can be used for brainstorming sales ideas, including:

- Could you exaggerate the product benefit to make it more forceful? Make it bigger? Multiply by twenty?
- Could a contradictory statement be used to emphasize the benefit?
- Could you make a before-and-after comparison to illustrate the benefit?
- What historical facts could be tied in to make the product benefit more memorable?
- Can you rewrite a proverb or saying into a memorable statement of the product benefit?
- Can you think of a context where the product or service would be startling or surprising?
- Can you compare the new product with something familiar to make the benefit immediately obvious?

There are dozens of other excellent guides to brainstorming and creativity,[88] all derived from the same basic ideas: to set aside some time for brainstorming, to set a clear goal, to be open and accepting, and to play around with lots of ideas. If your schedule and budget do not allow enough time for team brainstorming meetings, you can adapt the procedures from the guides to do it yourself. It won't be as good as a team meeting, but it's better than nothing.

For example, a brainstorming session on how to come up with more prospects to buy life insurance might produce a list that starts like this:

- Join the Chamber of Commerce.
- Research professional organizations.
- Ask customers for referrals.
- Get names from your neighbors, your lawyer, and your accountant.
- Send a fax introducing yourself before you make cold calls.
- Come up with an opening for cold calls that generates interest.
- Give speeches.
- Offer a free review of current coverage.

Some of these ideas are better than others. But if you start evaluating while you brainstorm, you will reduce the size of your own list. The key to success is to focus first on generating as many ideas as you can, and making sure that you have a long and rich list before you start evaluating.

As explained in the Introduction, encouraging creativity is an important component of our formal process, especially in Step 2 (Brainstorm with 26 AdverSelling principles). When the list is complete, then we pick the best in Step 3 (Define your AdverSelling activity). The real test happens in Step 4 (Test and improve) when you try it out with clients. If the first one you pick doesn't work, go back to the list and try another.

Reminders

- List as many ideas as you can to achieve a sales objective. Do not evaluate, just list them all.
- Don't just think about how to make small changes, think about doing things differently.
- Carry the list around for a few days, and add to it whenever you can.
- If you want group feedback, hold an office brainstorming meeting, following the guidelines above.
- After your list is complete, go back to pick the best ideas and try them in the field.

Ask yourself

- Am I stuck in a rut doing the same old thing?
- How could creativity improve my approach to sales?
- Could a brainstorming session help me find a new way to sell?

"The cure for boredom is curiosity.
There is no cure for curiosity."
— Ellen Parr

Chapter 9

_____

Stimulate curiosity

Humans are curious by nature, even nosy in some cases.
Psychologists have found this trait in other animals as
well. Chimps, pigeons, and rats will invest significant
energy into solving puzzles and manipulating latches,
with no apparent reward except the satisfaction of
finding a solution.

Advertisers took advantage of this curious streak in the
campaign for Clairol hair coloring: "Does she...or doesn't
she? Only her hairdresser knows for sure."

Clairol had been sold in the US since the 1930s, but had
trouble increasing sales because in that simpler time hair
coloring was "associated with actresses, models, and fast
women."[89] In 1955, Clairol launched a campaign to give
hair dye a natural and wholesome image. Clairol models
were pictured with ordinary clothes and little makeup,
and with children. Hair color ads traditionally ran in
fashion magazines like *Vogue* and *Harper's Bazaar*. The
Clairol ads ran in a middle American mainstay: *Life*
magazine.

The campaign helped increase Clairol's sales from $3
million in 1955 to $84 million in 1969. During that same
period, the US market for hair coloring increased from
$25 million to $136 million, while the proportion of
American women who colored their hair went from seven
percent to almost fifty percent.[90]

The idea of stimulating curiosity came from Shirley Polykoff, who was the only female copywriter at her ad agency when the campaign started. In her memoir, Polykoff explained that the slogan might be traced to her first dinner with her in-laws. When Shirley anxiously asked future husband George about his mother's reaction, he replied: "She thought you painted your hair."

Shirley did not admit it to George or his mother, but she was indeed a bottle blonde. And when she first analyzed this historic moment, she imagined that her mother-in-law might have thought "Does she or doesn't she?" and so in a way "maybe my mother-in-law wrote the line."[91] Despite this inauspicious start, Shirley proceeded to win fame, fortune, and George. She ultimately opened her own agency and was inducted into the Advertising Writer's Hall of Fame in 1973.[92]

One of the most clever series of ads built on curiosity came from Burma Shave in the 1920s. At that time, there were few cars and little competition for attention as people drove along the highway. When Clinton Odell introduced a new shaving cream, his son suggested that they take advantage of this boredom by building a series of consecutive roadside signs, spaced far enough apart that drivers had time to wonder what would be on the next one.[93]

Each sign had a single line from a homespun poem such as:

> Within this vale
> Of toil and sin
> Your head grows bald
> But not your chin
> Burma Shave

He had the ring
He had the flat
But she felt his chin
And that was that
Burma Shave

Doesn't kiss you
Like she useter?
Perhaps she's seen
A smoother rooster
Burma Shave

Don't stick your elbow
Out so far
It might go home
In another car
Burma Shave

The brand became a national success, and new billboards went up through the 1960s.

Applying the principle

In sales, stimulating curiosity can be especially helpful in building long term relationships.

For example, in many financial services firms, sales people are required to keep in touch with their biggest accounts on a predefined schedule. One of our Fortune 500 customers requires every investment counselor to call the top ten percent of their customers once per quarter.

But many sales people struggle with what to say in these calls. And a call that annoys a client is worse than no call at all.

One answer is to stimulate curiosity, perhaps with a voice mail message that includes this:

"I just saw a report of some research that I thought you might be interested in about trends in retirement saving and financial security. If you'd like to hear about some of the results, give me a call, or send me an email and I'll send you the link."

To prepare for when people call back, the investment counselor could create a fact sheet of talking points, like this:

- In 2004, The Employee Benefit Research Institute published a survey of over one thousand Americans, reporting that most people are not saving enough for retirement, and there's been very little change in retirement attitudes and behaviors over the last few years.
- Only about forty percent of Americans have actually tried to calculate how much they will need to retire comfortably.
- And even the ones who did the calculation sometimes ignore it. About a third of them could not even remember the results of the calculation.
- The reason this is important is that a calculation can change people's behavior and make them save more.
- About four out of ten people do save differently after they complete such an analysis.
- The article is called "Will Americans Ever Become Savers?" and a summary can be found on their web page www.ebri.org,[94] or I could fax you a copy.
- Would you like help doing an up-to-the-minute calculation of your retirement savings needs?

This particular article seems especially likely to get people talking about their own retirement plans. It also has the benefit of being unthreatening. If a client has never done a retirement calculation, this study says she has plenty of company.

The resulting discussion will not only advance the relationship by stimulating curiosity, it will also position the investment counselor as more than just a sales person, but as an expert who is aware of financial trends and a valued source for future help and advice.

Where can you find thought provoking facts like this that fit your product and your customers? The example above came from an eight minute Google search for "retirement plan research."[95]

Company newsletters may be helpful, and mass media and trade publications will be a source of countless fascinating factoids. You just need to keep an eye out for them, and make a copy or rip out the page when you see one. For financial services, that means starting with publications like the *Wall Street Journal, Business Week,* and *Fortune.* If you sell technical products, your best source could be *Wireless Week, GeoSpatial Solutions, Biophotonics International,* or any of the trade publications available from such websites as www.tradepub.com.

Stimulating curiosity works best as a low key approach to build relationships, rather than as a direct and immediate attempt to sell. If the interesting fact is that your new split dollar insurance policy can lead to significant savings, that is less likely to induce relationship-building curiosity, and more likely to be perceived as just another annoying sales call.

Reminders

- Collect facts and figures that would interest your clients, and use them to stimulate conversations.
- See if the U.S. Government has any interesting statistics you could use in presentations.
- List business and trade publications that might contain facts that would interest your customers.
- Test your facts on a few typical customers, to make sure they seem fascinating to your target audience.
- When you quote facts, be precise.
- Always be prepared with backup.
- If someone wants more information, quickly email or fax them your source.

Ask yourself

- Are there any facts about my product that could provoke curiosity?
- Are new technologies in the pipeline that my clients may be interested in?
- How could I collect more interesting facts about industry trends, and use them to engage prospects' interest?
- Should I set aside time for web research to try to find facts to stimulate curiosity?

"It's easier to go up into the mountains to catch tigers than to ask others for help."
– Chinese proverb.

Chapter **10**

Ask for help

Who can prevent forest fires? That's right. Smokey Bear says *only you* can prevent forest fires. According to the Smokey Bear Home Page, a study of American school children found that "Only you can prevent forest fires" was more familiar than any other advertising slogan. So don't play with matches or leave a camp fire unattended.

Smokey's origins can be traced to a World War II public service campaign with the slogan: "Careless Matches Aid the Axis – Prevent Forest Fires." East Coast posters included a caricature of a threatening Adolph Hitler, West Coast posters used Japanese Prime Minister Tojo Hideki. But market research on both coasts suggested the need for a kinder gentler approach, and in 1944, Smokey Bear was born.

Smokey's big break came in 1950 when a fire started by pesky humans burned seventeen thousand acres in the Capitan Mountains in New Mexico. A little bear cub scampered up a tree, and was rescued by firefighters. At a vet's office in Santa Fe, a photographer dabbed some honey on the chin of the warden's daughter, and took a photo of the cub licking it off. The cub became a star, was named Smokey, and moved to the National Zoo in Washington, DC.

Smokey never seemed happy in our nation's capital.[96] He was a quiet loner, never as popular as later National Zoo stars such as Ling Ling the Panda. He refused to mate with Goldie Bear, a mail order bride flown in from New Mexico.

Many ad campaigns succeed by asking people for help.

Smokey got arthritis and died, cubless, in 1976. His body was returned to the Smokey Bear Historical Park near the site of the forest fire, in an area described on his unofficial website as "the heart of the beautiful downtown Capitan." The zip code is "Smokey Bear 20252." At the gift shop, you can buy many of the 160 official Smokey Bear products ranging from bubble bath to charcoal briquettes. At his peak, Smokey earned the US Forest Service $250,000 per year in royalties.

Smokey is the longest running campaign in the history of the Ad Council, a nonprofit group that develops public service ads with volunteer help, and arguably its most successful. In 1944, thirty million acres were destroyed by US forest fires every year. By 1990, this had declined to 5.4 million, despite the increase in the population.[97]

But all good things must pass, and in the last few years there's been a Smokey backlash. Many forest ecologists now argue that some forest fires are necessary.

Many ad campaigns like Smokey's have succeeded because they asked people for help. A few years ago, did you vote in the campaign to choose new colors for M&Ms? At a minimum, it probably caught your attention. And if they picked your color, it probably made you more likely to go out and try the new ones.

Applying the principle

Most people like to be helpful, and sales professionals can ask for help from many different sources, including friends, strangers, customers, peers, and managers.

You might think that the best approach to networking is to directly ask everyone you meet, "How can you help me?" But in the book *Endless Referrals*, Bob Burg suggests that instead you should focus on "How can I help you?" He notes that, when all things are equal, people prefer to do business with others whom they know, like, and trust. Done properly, networking will expand the number of people who know, like, and trust you.

The implications of Burg's approach are clear and dramatic. If you meet someone new at a business networking event, Burg advises you to: "Invest 99.9 percent of the conversation asking that person questions about herself and her business. Do not talk about you and your business." Ask the person to describe their ideal customer, and then see if you can help them find some new ones.

There will certainly be times when it is legitimate and productive to ask for help directly. In Burg's approach, these occasions will emerge naturally as you develop mutually beneficial relationships. "Networking involves giving to others and helping them succeed in their lives and careers. When accomplished in a pragmatic and organized fashion, we find that we get back what we put out tenfold, both personally and professionally."[98]

Other approaches to networking stress the importance of actively seeking referrals from satisfied customers. For professional service firms like law and accounting, referrals can be the single most important source of worthwhile leads. But referrals don't come quickly; they must be earned over time.

Some people are much more liberal with referrals than others. When you find one, work hard to keep that source happy, and to keep giving you referrals. According to this view, if you don't ask for customer referrals, you shall not receive them.

Some successful professionals are masters at directly asking customers for help in getting their business. They never submit a completed proposal, but always first ask for help reviewing a draft, to make sure that the proposal meets the client's needs, and to get a chance to fix errors or misconceptions before they become serious. This can also be a good way to build relationships, and to give you an excuse to keep in touch.

Your peers, the people you work with every day, are another valuable source of help. The help could be minor, such as looking over a letter or proposal before you send it out, just to get another set of eyes looking at it. Or it could be as major as a mentoring relationship, when an experienced person takes a new employee under her wing. Again, if you want this kind of help, it all starts when you ask.

Last but certainly not least, ask for help from your management. Your definition of top management will obviously depend on your company and your situation. If you are trying to explain why the next quarter will be so much better than the last one, your audience could be as high as the CEO or the Board. If you're discussing your child's homework, it's probably your spouse. But whoever your senior management may be, it is always wise to work for their support.

Your manager wants you to succeed. If you look good, she looks good. But she's really busy, because she has a lot of meetings to go to. So if you want more than the usual support, you are going to have to ask for it. Ask directly: how you can help her, how she can help you, and how does her management define success?

Some sales people stay at a single company for many years by treating their manager as their most important client, the one who can cut off a pay check. An occasional lunch to discuss concerns and hot buttons may surprise you and lead to changes in your activities.

Maybe you think your manager doesn't have time for you, because she is too busy working with new employees and problem personnel. If that's true, she is making a mistake.

The most successful sales managers maximize their impact on revenue by spending most of their time with top producers, not with problem employees. Even when top people don't need help or advice, they may need an audience. A manager's presence "brings out the best in your stars, in much the same way that athletic teams play better in front of the home crowd."[99]

In large organizations, the best sales people may need the manager to serve as a buffer, to run interference with the home office while they can focus on getting more meetings and closing more deals. Sometimes, the most valuable help you can ask for is to be left alone.

Reminders

- Don't just ask for help, offer help to others.
- Ask customers directly: What would I have to say to sell you my product?
- Build relationships by asking for professional help on something that is not directly related to sales, such as responding to a survey. But if you tell people that it is not for sales, live up to your promise, and stay away from sales in that call.
- Ask yourself how you can help your colleagues, and how they can help you.
- Identify situations where management support can help you increase sales.
- Ask your sales manager:
  - What can I do better?
  - How can I help you?
  - How can you help me?

Ask yourself

- How could I enlist people's natural tendency to be helpful?
- Should I be more active in seeking out referrals?
- Have I asked any clients for advice lately?
- Do I know exactly how my management defines success?
- How could my manager help me?
- How could I make my manager look good?
- How have I shown management that I am trying to achieve their goals?

> *"Fashion is a social agreement…the result of a*
> *consensus of a large group of people."*
> *– Stella Blum*

Chapter 11

Build consensus

Most people want to fit in. You see it in second grade when only one brand of sneakers will do, and you see it in the senior center when everyone's arts and crafts use the same color schemes.

Advertisers often build on the desire to conform, as when American citizens were urged to buy war bonds in World War II with such slogans as "Help Defend Your Country," "Protect Your Personal Future," "Back the Attack," and "Doing All You Can, Brother?" By the end of the war, eighty-five million Americans, well over half the population, had purchased over $180 billion in War Bonds.[100] In this case, the advertisers did not need to build a consensus that Hitler was bad, they just had to tap into it with the message, "We're all in this together."

Have you ever watched the audience reaction in a TV infomercial? When the miracle product is first introduced, the audience looks skeptical. The pitchman asks: "Would you believe it if I told you this same rotisserie that just cooked a turkey could also be used to dry your hair?" A surprised murmur rises from the audience, as the camera pans their skeptical faces. But when Heather shows how well it dries her blond hair, the *nos* turn to *oohs* and *ahs* of amazement. Spontaneous applause erupts. The tribe has spoken.

The "Just Say No" campaign to combat illicit drugs was also built around this concept.[101] In 1985, First Lady Nancy Reagan inspired three elementary school children to start the first "Just Say No" club. The campaign was aimed at children seven to fourteen, and was built around the "Three Steps to Say No."

Step 1: Figure out if what your friend wants to do is OK.
Step 2: If it is wrong, say "No."
Step 3: Suggest other things to do instead.

Social modeling and pressure can powerfully influence behavior.

The Topsville company licensed the slogan for children's sportswear, and mothers could buy items ranging from shirts and shorts to sweatpants and skirts with "Just Say No" printed in several languages. The message was printed on milk cartons and published in newspaper and TV ads. Within a few years ten thousand Just Say No clubs had been formed with over two hundred thousand members.

When there was a significant decline in illicit drug use in the 1980s, proponents argued that this campaign had contributed to that downward trend.

Social psychologists have published thousands of studies showing how social pressure can influence people's reactions. If you've taken even a single psychology class, you may remember Solomon Asch's classic studies of conformity. Asch assembled groups of seven people and told them they were in a study on perception. In fact, the study was on group pressure, and only one person in each group of seven was an experimental subject, the other six worked for Asch.

The entire group sat around a table and looked at two cards, one with a single "standard line," the other with three "comparison lines" of varying lengths. The task was simple: each person was to pick out the comparison line that matched the standard. They went around the table and each person gave their answer aloud.

At first, it seemed trivially easy. The differences between the lines were easy to spot, and all seven people agreed time after time. But then they got to a comparison designed to test the will power of the one person who was actually the experimental subject. In this case, anyone could see that line 2 matched the comparison line. But the first person said "1." So did the second person, the third, the fourth, and the fifth. By the time they got to the experimental subject, sitting in the sixth chair, he wondered who was going crazy: the other five people or himself.

Note that there was no reward for agreement; the only reason to give the wrong answer was a desire to fit in. Under these circumstances, the social pressure to give the wrong answer led thirty-seven percent to ignore their eyes and go with the crowd. Asch noted that while two thirds resisted the pressure, the fact that one third conformed was troubling: "That reasonably intelligent and well meaning young people are willing to call white black is a matter of concern."

Many studies followed, with so many variations that you can now take an advanced psychology course on the factors that influence conformity and obedience. What's important from our perspective is that social modeling and social pressure have a powerful influence on behavior.

Applying the principle

If you are selling a six-figure consulting solution or software system, you know that it's going to take a while. And you know that the sales process is often a long and winding road, with many false starts, dead ends, and rapid mood swings. That's just the nature of large sales:

there are many people on the other side of the table, and they don't always agree. Whenever one of them tells you something, it must be weighed against what the others may think.

Robert Miller and Stephen Heiman developed the "Strategic Selling" system to build consensus in this challenging environment. They identified several distinct buying influences in the complex sale, including:

- The *Economic Buying Influence* – the alpha dog who controls the money, and is the ultimate decision maker. This buyer may or may not want the lowest price, but is always looking for the best return on investment.

- The *User Buying Influence* – exerted by one or many people who will actually use the product or service. Sales beginners often deal only with users, and are surprised to find these users don't always have the power to buy what they want.

- The *Technical Buying Influence* – concerned with measurable and quantifiable standards and specifications which the organization may have for a particular product. This group has the negative veto power to prevent purchases that don't conform to company standards, but rarely has the positive power to force a purchase.

- The *Coach* – an insider who can help a sales person build consensus by providing information and interpreting events as the situation develops.

The coach can help you blow away the smoke to find who really makes the decision, and what they care about. The coach usually works for the buyer and is always someone whose interests are aligned with yours.

Miller and Heiman[102] list four main ways that a good coach can help build consensus by helping you:

- Figure out who the real key players in this buying decision really are (in a large organization, they are often different from the people who believe they are the real players)

- Identify which of your strengths will have the biggest impact in this situation

- Predict how different buyers may react to your proposal, based on their different perspectives

- Understand the results that each buyer needs to see your proposal as a win-win.

While every large sale includes economic, technical, and user influences, the only way to have a coach is to find someone whose interests are aligned with yours, and to build the role. Nobody said this would be easy. But a coach who believes the sale will benefit both her company and herself will be an enormous help in building consensus not just for this sale, but for the next one.

Reminders

- With large groups, try to figure out what they agree on, and work from there.
- Identify the needs of each sub-group and search for common ground.
- If there are several factions, establish a bond with each one.
- In complex sales, try to find someone whose interests align with yours, and who can serve as an inside coach to keep you on track throughout the long sales process.

Ask yourself

- Who are the stakeholders within the customer organization?
- What are the primary needs of each stakeholder?
- How can I create consensus, and build on it?

> *"We don't want to over-stimulate these people.*
> *They just had pudding."*
> — *Nursing home employee in TV show "The Simpsons"*

Chapter **12**

Personalize and customize

A single size suit will not fit everyone, and a single message will not fit every subgroup in your audience.

The need for multiple messages is most obvious when advertising goes global. When Anheuser Busch first began promoting Budweiser beer in China, they used an ad that had been quite popular in the US. A line of ants was shown carrying a Bud, then pouring it into their ant hill. Then the party music was turned up ("Do a little dance, make a little love, get down tonight . . ."), and the ground began to shake from the fun. But Chinese viewers did not recognize the commotion as a party for ants; they thought Budweiser was a pesticide.

The notion of adjusting the message to each subgroup has led to an entire field of "ethnic advertising." Companies see huge opportunities in selling their products in minority markets, which are the fastest growing segments of the population. Between 1990 and 2000, while the US white population grew by about six percent, the African-American and black population increased by sixteen percent, Asian-American by forty-eight percent, and US Hispanic by fifty-eight percent. Many believe that ethnic advertising, designed by people who are themselves part of the target group and totally familiar with its culture, is the most effective way to reach these groups.[103]

Even the government uses ethnic marketing. For the
2000 Census, they hired the Bravo Group, a division of
Young & Rubicam, to create a Spanish version of the
census slogan "It's our future – don't leave it blank." The
successful campaign was built around the translation
"hagase contar," which can be translated "get yourself
counted" or "make yourself count." The ads stressed that
census information was confidential, could not be used to
deport undocumented aliens, and would make a
difference to their political power and the education of
their children.[104]

Some companies create separate products for different sub-groups.

Advertising Age's annual review of industry statistics
includes charts of the top ten "multicultural agencies
marketing to Hispanics" (led by the Bravo Group with US
gross income of $26 million) and the top ten "marketing
to African-Americans" (led by "Global Hue" with $30
million).[105]

In 2003, Procter & Gamble spent $90 million on
advertising specifically directed at Latinos for twelve
products, including Crest and Tide, and also modified the
products themselves to "tailor everything from detergent
to toothpaste to Latino tastes."[106]

Or consider the way Tommy Hilfiger has followed several
decades worth of fads to customize its products to
changing tastes. Tommy first succeeded in 1969 as a
hippie entrepreneur in Elmira, New York. Elmira
suffered from a bell bottom shortage, so Tommy drove to
New York City, bought bell bottoms in bulk, resold them
back home in upstate New York, and founded a chain of
stores with the 60s name, "People's Place."

Unfortunately, they went bankrupt in 1975, and Tommy
moved on to a period of creating disco fashions for
Jordache.[107]

In 1985, he started his own fashion company, and invested heavily in youth advertising and promotions. His breakthrough came in 1994 when Snoop Doggy Dog wore a red, white, and blue Hilfiger shirt on *Saturday Night Live.* Some believe that this appearance alone generated $90 million in sales,[108] and led to more free Hilfiger clothes for Coolio, TLC, the Fugees, and many others. However he accomplished it, Tommy Hilfiger has succeeded in speaking the language of youth to the tune of nearly two billion dollars in annual sales.

Traditional advertising customizes to large sub-groups. But new technology can take personalization a step further with "one-to-one marketing," including ads tailored to each individual's interests. For example, computers could track the fact that you often visit websites about fly-fishing, and live in Michigan. Within minutes, your email inbox could include announcements about the latest breakthroughs in spey rods designed for Great Lakes streams and rivers.

The success of internet search advertising is also related to "personalize and customize." When you click on one of those little ads that appear on the right side of the page when you type a term in Google, you are pre-selecting yourself as an interested audience. The search engine advertising business has grown from essentially zero in 1999, to $3.9 billion in 2003. Spending on search-based ads is projected to continue to grow rapidly for the next few years, anywhere from twenty to fifty percent per year.[109]

Concerns about spam and privacy have slowed the growth of some types of internet advertising, but marketing visionaries remain optimistic about a future in which technology will personalize and customize the ads you see.

Applying the principle

Personalization and customization always begins with knowledge about each individual.

The knowledge can be on the surface level, using the family photos on your client's desk as a conversation starter. Many experienced pros keep track of personal info in their database, and use it to maintain an ongoing phone or email relationship. The conversation always feels more civilized if it begins with small talk about your client's pit bull or bass fishing trophy.

A little personalization can go a long way. That's why proposal writers so often add the logo from the client's web page; it creates a warm feeling that you are customizing your presentation (even if the rest of the proposal is the same for every client).

At a deeper level, personalization and customization leads to a never ending quest for more information about what clients care about, and why. Systems like *Consultative Selling* are built around asking questions to determine a client's "pain," and relating that pain to your product solution.

Here, the key to success is to ask the right questions in the right way. In the book *Stop Telling, Start Selling*, Linda Richardson[110] uses the anagram DROP-INS to distinguish seven different types of questions used in sales:

- **D**ecision-Making questions, such as "Who else will be involved in deciding whether to purchase our service?"
- **R**elationship questions, such as "Are you satisfied with our performance in past projects?"
- **O**perational questions, such as "How many people are in your department?"
- **P**roblem questions, such as "Where do you think your current system could be improved?"

- Interpersonal questions, such as "Where do you play golf?"
- Need questions, such as "What would you like to accomplish with this project?"
- Strategy questions, such as "Is this project related to the company's long-term goals?"

If you've had a successful career in sales, you're already good at asking questions. But it never hurts to get a little better (see also Chapter 4 Add Value and Chapter 5 Listen). Given genuine curiosity, anyone can be a great questioner. But even the best require preparation to keep the questions on track to take the shortest possible path to the sale.

Reminders

- Work hard to understand each prospect's unique requirements, and adjust your sales message accordingly.
- Keep a file of personal information – from birthdays to hobbies – and use it for keeping in touch.
- Send occasional handwritten notes to reinforce personal connections.
- Make eye contact.
- Divide prospects into groups, based on their needs. For example, brokers distinguish between singles, marrieds with and without kids, and retired.
- Adapt benefits statements to the needs of each group.
- Ask lots of questions so that you are sure you understand each individual's unique point of view.
- For a group presentation, collect information in advance about the needs and hot buttons of the decision maker and recommenders.
- Remind yourself: proposals don't sell, people do.

Ask yourself

- Do I present information in a standardized way, when I could be customizing it to each person or group?
- Do I take sufficient time to get to know individual customers' needs so that I can personalize and customize?
- Do my customers fall into a few obvious groups with different needs?
- How can I get a better understanding of the differences in their concerns and interests?
- How can I adapt my message to each group?
- What do prospects want from my presentation?
- What will they do with my information?
- Do I add a personal element to every communication?

"I am not a role model."
– Charles Barkley

Chapter 13

Quote testimonials

A few years ago, George Foreman's Lean Mean Grilling Machine was at the top of my Christmas list. My daughter Eileen and I love infomercials, and when George Foreman showed how much fat poured out of a hamburger,[111] we just had to have one.

Once I got my grill, the biggest surprise was my wife's reaction. No fan of infomercials, Pat had mocked my choice of appliance. But within a few days she became the grill's biggest fan.

Pat's favorite meal is anything prepared by someone else, and cooking on the grill is the next best thing to not cooking at all. Just put in your dinner, and a few minutes later sit down to a satisfying fat-reduced meal. To this day in the Hassett household, every chicken breast, every salmon filet, and every swordfish steak cooks only on the Lean Mean Grilling Machine.

Since I first wrote about this, I have lost count of the people who have come up to me to say that they had tried the grill after reading my book. Why? They didn't know me and they didn't know my wife. But then again, I didn't know George, and he's gone on to become one of the most successful pitchmen of this generation.

George's success may have something to do with his selectivity. Although he's been offered deals to endorse over two hundred products, as these words are written he's agreed to only four: the Grill, Meinicke Mufflers, Con Agra meats, and most recently the Casual Male Big & Tall clothes chain.[112]

Testimonials produce confidence and belief, whether from celebrities, experts, or ordinary people. Psychologists have observed this phenomenon over and over, as when Pratkanis and Aronson reported that "a beautiful woman – simply because she was beautiful – could have a major impact on the opinions of an audience."[113]

Testimonial equivalents even work in the animal kingdom.[114] In one study, when new foods were introduced into a troop of Japanese monkeys, the preference spread slowly through the group if the first tasters were nerd-like low status monkeys. But when new foods were first given to the football quarterback-type alpha monkey leaders, the foods became popular within hours.

Similarly, in the mid-90s when Michael Jordan started eating three Energy Booster bars before each game, the rest of the team quickly followed. Interestingly, Chicago Bull non-stars Steve Kerr and B. J. Armstrong had been eating three Energy Booster bars for some time. But it was only after Mike started that the rest of the team followed.

Jordan was also the star of several of the longest lasting and most successful celebrity endorsement ads of all time, including Nike's Just Do It campaign, Hanes underwear, and drinking Gatorade to "Be Like Mike." Near his peak, *Fortune* magazine estimated Jordan's value as an advertising icon at ten billion dollars.[115] That's right, ten billion – $5.2 billion in marketing value to Nike alone.

There are two major schools of thought about testimonials. One is to stick to celebrities, the Michael Jordans and George Foremans of the world. Others favor the principle of similarity: the more similar your endorsers are to your audience, the more credible they will be.

Evidence supporting this view can be found in many psychological experiments, including a 1960s classic in which Columbia psychologists left "lost wallets" in mid-town Manhattan.[116]

Endorsers are more credible when they are similar to the audience.

Each wallet contained a check for $26.30 plus two dollars in cash, and was wrapped in an envelope addressed to the owner. In the fictional scenario these psychologists created, the wallet was lost twice: first by the original owner, and then by someone who had planned to return it. Half of the wallets included letters written in broken English, which identified the finder as a recent immigrant. The other half included letters which seemed to have been written by an average New Yorker.

People were more likely to imitate the letter writer and drop the wallet in a mailbox when the first finder seemed to be someone like them. Seventy percent of the wallets were returned with the average person letters, but only thirty-three percent with the "immigrant" letters. This is just one of many studies suggesting that you are more likely to follow someone else's lead if you perceive them as "just like me."

Procter & Gamble has been a particularly big believer in the principle of similarity. They've based commercials on testimonials from ordinary people from the hidden camera ads for Folger's instant coffee, to those annoying letters from detergent fans who can't wait to tell how Cheer removed their laundry stains.[117]

Do you think that testimonials will become less effective as the American population becomes more educated and sophisticated? The evidence suggests otherwise. When *Advertising Age* studied the effectiveness of ads in 2002, "Showcased celebrities played a major role in two-thirds of the twenty most-remembered TV ads," including

Britney Spears, Austin Powers, Kirstie Alley, Jason Alexander, Barry Bonds, and Michael Jordan.[118]

The most amazing thing to me is how powerful testimonials can be even when they come from the very people who are selling. Some infomercial companies keep overhead down by hawking their own products, starting with the father of infomercials, Ron Popeil. In 1964, Popeil bought some late night TV time to sell a spray gun attachment he had invented to perform a variety of household tasks: "It washes. It waxes. It kills bugs," he gushed.[119] And the rest is history.

Popeil's career extended over several decades, including "Great Looking Hair" spray-on kits to cover bald spots. Five hundred thousand kits were sold in the first seven months. Popeil made (and lost) several fortunes selling the Veg-O-Matic vegetable slicer, the Popeil Pasta/ Sausage Maker, the Ronco Food Dehydrator, the smokeless ashtray, and the Pocket Fisherman (a fishing rod that can attach to your belt).[120]

Infomercials have grown to become a multibillion dollar industry with their own trade association (the ERA – Electronic Retailing Association – at www.retailing.org). All built on a foundation of testimonials with sellers pitching their own products.

Applying the principle

If your product literature already includes testimonials, it may be simply a matter of calling attention to them. For example, you could add a clickable link to your email signature that says: To see what clients say about our "totally different and refreshing approach" that "will increase sales," go to _____.

If your personal service is an important selling point, you also might want to collect additional quotes that tell specific stories about how you helped particular clients.

If you've ever tried to get testimonials, you probably found that even though you have plenty of customers who love your product and your service, it's hard to get good quotes from them. You will need patience and persistence, but the payoff can be enormous. And it will get easier if you follow the advice below.

There are two critical steps: Find people who would like to be quoted, and make it easy for them to give you a useful quote.

If you have lots of customers and good service, it won't be hard to find people, it just takes a little time to work with them.

To maximize the credibility of the quotes, you should include each person's full name and title. This may lead you to focus on the customers with the most impressive titles and affiliations. You definitely want to aim high. If people turn you down, no one else will ever know.

If you provide some sort of evaluation survey for post-sales follow-up, you could add a standard question such as: "Can we quote you on our web page and marketing materials?" Or add a direct request to letters and emails that you send after the sale.

Some percentage of your clients will be thrilled to be quoted, and later to see their name in your brochure or on the web. Which also gives you a good excuse to keep in touch with them.

Once you have found a candidate, the next step is to make it easy to be quoted. This process must be played by ear, and adapted to each person. Some may be offended if they think you are trying to put words in their mouth. Others will be thrilled to approve a quote that sounds good and took little effort, as long as it's based on their verbal comments.

One very effective strategy is to say: "Many of the people we've worked with prefer to start with a short interview about what they liked. Then I'll draft a quote, and you can review it to make sure I've correctly captured your ideas."

And don't forget the principle of similarity: the more similar your endorsers are to your audience, the more credible they will be. If you are trying to convince sales professionals, don't quote Harvard Professors, unless they happen to specialize in sales and will seem credible to your target audience.

Reminders

- Before you start collecting quotes, decide what marketing message you want to reinforce.
- Pick credible sources, and aim high.
- Interview people about what they like, then offer to summarize what they said in a few pithy quotes.
- If they accept, use their wording, submit your version for approval, and expect changes.
- Keep quotes short.
- Always use full names and titles.
- Keep your list fresh by adding new quotes, and rotating which ones are featured.
- Keep a file with the emails or notes providing final approval of each quote.
- Avoid the suspicious ellipsis (extra periods that indicate you've removed some words, like this . . .).

Ask yourself

- Can I use existing company testimonials more effectively?
- Should I incorporate testimonials into routine correspondence?
- Should I devote more time to collecting quotes from satisfied customers?
- If clients rely on my personal service (as they do for brokers and insurance agents), should I collect testimonials specifically about me?
- Who would be most credible to my customers?

*"The slogan...abolishes reflection: the slogan
does not argue, it asserts and commands."*
– Johan Huizinga

Chapter 14

Use a slogan

Slogans can be powerful selling tools. Table 4 lists the
top ten slogans of the twentieth century, according to
Advertising Age. How many do you recognize?

When Avis started saying in 1962, "We try harder," the
company had not posted a profit in fifteen years. Avis
President Robert Townshend issued a challenge to
advertisers: he needed five million dollars worth of
impact, on a one million dollar budget. Bill Bernbach of
Doyle Dane Bernbach accepted the challenge, based on
one condition: Avis had to "promise to run everything we
write without changing a bloody comma."[121]

Bernbach's "We try harder" ads violated at least two laws
of 1960s advertising: they mentioned a competitor, and
they were honest. Copywriter Paula Green later reported
that the campaign "almost didn't run . . . . It made a lot of
people uncomfortable. It even irritated a lot of people
here [at the ad agency]. It researched miserably."[122]

But of course Avis ran the "We try harder" ads, and in the
first year went from a loss of $3.2 million to a profit of
$1.2 million. The slogan has been repeated for more than
forty years. In one of the first ads, CEO Robert
Townsend was described as "a nut about keeping in
touch." The ad included his phone number, and urged
dissatisfied customers to call. Townsend received many
calls, but every single one was a compliment, which

reinforced customers' commitment to the brand. When Avis became an employee-owned company in 1987, the tag line was temporarily adapted to "Owners try harder."[123] Then they went back to the original.

TABLE 4

TOP 10 SLOGANS OF THE 20ᵀᴴ CENTURY

1. Diamonds are forever (De Beers)

2. Just do it (Nike)

3. The pause that refreshes (Coca-Cola)

4. Tastes great, less filling (Miller Lite)

5. We try harder (Avis)

6. Good to the last drop (Maxwell House)

7. Breakfast of champions (Wheaties)

8. Does she…or doesn't she? (Clairol)

9. When it rains it pours (Morton Salt)

10. Where's the beef? (Wendy's)

Source: Garfield, Bob. "Top 100 Advertising Campaigns of the Century." *Advertising Age.* www.adage.com/century/slogans.html

---

One of the things that makes the Avis slogan so effective is the fact that it struck a chord with customers and felt true. Hertz might get away with being complacent, but as the underdog, Avis would indeed be motivated to try harder.

Applying the principle

Should you use your company's slogan more? They paid a lot of money to create, test, and repeat that message. Could you derive more value from that investment?

Whether your company uses a memorable slogan or not, you could create a selling slogan for your team or for yourself, such as: *E-mail me any time.*

- My cell phone is always on.
- We will make you very very happy.
- I can fix it.
- I sell money.[124]

The "I sell money" slogan came from an insurance agent, who says "It sounds a little hokey, but it works." When people ask what it means, he explains: "When it's time to retire or go to college, I'll send you money. If there's a death, I'll send you money. If you're disabled, I'll send you money."

You may need to experiment with a few selling slogans to find one that resonates with your customers. But when you have a slogan that works, you can use it everywhere, from business cards to voice mail to email.

Another interesting way to apply this principle is to create a personal slogan, to motivate yourself or to focus your energy. Again, only you can create the slogan, because only you know what you need to work on. Here are a few examples:
- Try twenty-five things, one will work.
- It's a numbers game.
- Give it time.
- Listen.
- I can do it.

It's OK if your personal slogans are sappy or clichés. You're the only one who's listening.

Reminders

and website
^

- Use your company slogan on your business card, your email signature, and your voice mail message.
- Create a selling slogan for your product, and use it consistently.
- Ask other members of your team to use your selling slogan.
- Create a personal slogan to motivate yourself and direct your energy.
- Repeat positive personal slogans to yourself to stay upbeat.

Ask yourself

- Should I use a company slogan, a selling slogan, or a personal slogan?
- Will my selling slogan touch their hearts and stimulate their minds?
- Does my selling slogan address what my audience worries about?
- Will my personal slogan help me to stay motivated?

"What's in a brand?
A fifty-percent markup."
— Old marketing joke

Chapter 15

Build on the brand

Do you know why Santa Claus always wears red? To match the Coca-Cola logo.

Before the 1930s, nobody knew what Santa looked like. Sometimes artists portrayed him as tall and gaunt, sometimes as stocky. And his clothes came in many colors, including blue, yellow, and green.[125] But when Coke wanted to build an ad campaign around Santa, they needed a distinctive and standardized St. Nick.

Coke's "Thirst has no season" campaign had started a few years earlier to solve the problem of declining Coke sales every winter. They had some early success with images of skiers enjoying "the pause that refreshes." Then someone suggested adding the ultimate symbol of winter: Santa Claus himself. This would not only address the seasonal dip, it might also boost soda drinking in children, then a clear growth market.

Coke commissioned several artists to portray Santa, and chose Haddon Sundblom's image of a chubby bearded Santa wearing Coca-Cola red. From 1931 to 1964, every year Coke commissioned Sundblom to draw a different Santa enjoying a refreshing cola beverage – in the sleigh, on the roof between reindeer rides, or sitting in front of the fireplace relaxing before his next stop.

For several decades, all of America and the entire world saw Sundblom's generously proportioned red Santa on billboards, in magazines, and in newspapers. Over time, most people lost track of why this symbol of yuletide had started wearing red.[126]

Santa helped build the value of the Coca-Cola brand, which *Business Week* rated the number one brand in the world, with a value of $70 billion. Their analysis put a total value of over $350 billion in sales on the top ten global brands.[127]

One reason Coke is at the top of this list is that they have outspent competitors for over a century on advertising. By 1920, sodas like Orange Crush, Hires Root Beer, Hurty Peek Lemon, and others shared less than half the soft drink market; Coke had the rest. They continued to spend during the Depression, billing Coca-Cola as an affordable break from the harsh realities of daily life. It is only in the last few decades that Coke sales have begun to decline, as Pepsi mounted a stronger challenge, and carbonated drinks became less popular.

Coke may have the most valuable brand, but it is not the logo which is most often requested in tattoo parlors. That honor belongs to Harley-Davidson, which once claimed that over five percent of their customers had the Harley name inked into their skin.[128]

In the 1950s and 1960s, Harley controlled three-quarters of the motorcycle market. Then Honda introduced lightweight bikes which were more reliable and much less expensive. Harley lost money for a decade, until they rebuilt the brand for a new demographic: RUBs, or rich urban bikers. Once that transition was made, the Harley brand became associated with patriotism, personal freedom, and machismo, and Harley could not build bikes fast enough to meet demand.

TABLE 5

10 MOST VALUABLE BRANDS

1. Coca-Cola – $70 billion

2. Microsoft – $65 billion

3. IBM – $52 billion

4. GE – $42 billion

5. Intel – $31 billion

6. Nokia – $29 billion

7. Disney – $28 billion

8. McDonald's – $25 billion

9. Marlboro – $22 billion

10. Mercedes – $21 billion

Source: "Brands in an Age of Anti-Americanism." *Business Week* 4 August 2003: 69-79.

They not only recaptured over fifty percent of the market for heavyweight bikes, they started a new Motor Clothes division with advertising designed "to tap into the rebellious desires of the RUBs without alienating the hardcore biker audience." For example, one black and white photo showed a bearded guy you'd never mess with, complete with bandana, sunglasses, leather vest, patches, and chains. The headline: "The necktie is society's leash."[129]

The ads not only won awards, they led to over $100 million in annual sales of Harley protective leathers, T-shirts, jewelry, sweaters, socks, and swimwear.

Brands can live a very long time, in part because they take so long to establish. When researchers compared the leading brands of 1925 and 1985 in twenty-two product categories they found that nineteen of the twenty-two leaders were the same in both years.[130] Brands like Kodak cameras, Wrigley gum, Eveready batteries, Gillette razors, Singer sewing machines, Del Monte canned fruit, Lipton tea, and Campbell soup led their competitors in the 1920s, and they still led them sixty years later.

One of the most interesting uses of branding in recent years has been the drug company campaigns to get consumers to request drugs by name. According to a Harvard-MIT study, the drug industry spent $2.7 billion in 2001 on direct-to-consumer advertising. This is up from $800 million in 1996, and from nothing at all a few decades ago.

And it worked: every dollar that drug companies spent on ads increased sales by $4.20.[131] The number of purchased prescriptions rose seventy percent in the last decade, from two billion in 1993 to 3.4 billion in 2003.[132] The biggest drug brands are summarized in Table 6.

Interestingly, these researchers found that the ads boosted spending not just on the advertised brands, but also on their competitors. The ads are effective in getting allergy sufferers to ask the doctor for Claritin, for example, but doctors may still prescribe other medicines. The advertising still pays for itself, since sickness is a growth industry, and there's plenty of revenue to go around.

Branding may be most valuable for luxury brands such as Louis Vuitton, which Business Week described as "the most profitable luxury brand on the planet."[133] They never run a sale for the $190 Vuitton key holders, the

$730 Vuitton handbags, the $2,240 Pégase 60 suitcase, or any other Vuitton item, because they don't have to.

Vuitton says their success is based on quality and value: they test their zippers five thousand times, use only hides from Northern European cattle (which have few blemishes from insect bites), and offer lifetime free repairs. Some believe that much of the value is in the eye of the beholder, based on the marketing and mystique that starts with advertisements featuring Jennifer Lopez and Kate Moss. "You buy into the dream of Louis Vuitton," said one French consumer quoted in the Business Week article. "We're part of a sect, and the more they put their prices up, the more we come back. They pull the wool over our eyes, but we love it."[134]

TABLE 6

10 BEST SELLING PRESCRIPTION DRUGS

1. Lipitor (cholesterol) – $10.3 billion

2. Zocor (cholesterol) – $6.1 billion

3. Zyprexa (anti-psychotic) - $4.8 billion

4. Norvasc (blood pressure) - $4.5 billion

5. Procrit (anemia) – $4.0 billion

6. Prevacid (heartburn) – $4.0 billion

7. Nexium (heartburn) - $3.8 billion

8. Plavix (blood thinner) - $3.7 billion

9 Advair (asthma) - $3.7 billion

10. Zoloft (depression) – $3.4 billion

Source: Herper, Matthew, The World's Best-Selling Drugs, www.forbes.com/technology/2004/03/16/cx_mh_0316bestsell ing.html

---

In the very funny book *Living It Up,* James Twitchell argues that people are increasingly basing their personal identities on the brands they use: wearing Armani, carrying a Hermes bag and checking the time on a Philippe Patek watch. There's a luxury brand for everyone. If you can't afford Matteo or Frette Egyptian cotton, you can still buy five star bedding at K-Mart: the Martha Stewart Embroidered Tambour Collection.

Twitchell sees this growing commitment to luxury as a defining characteristic of the way we live: "If you want to understand material culture at the beginning of the twenty-first century, you must understand the overwhelming importance of unnecessary material . . . .You are what you consume."[135]

Applying the principle

How strong is your company's brand? Are you getting the full benefit of its power in your selling?

If the answer is no, consider re-acquainting yourself with the core brand identity on your brochures and web page. Maybe you've been working with the brand for so long that you've grown a little tired of it. But new prospects don't feel that way, and you would be wise to maximize your personal benefit from all those ads the company pays for.

Regardless of whether you need to do more with the company brand, there's another way this concept can be applied to your selling. Robert Krumroy's book *Identity Branding* lists many tips and techniques for creating a personal brand.[136] This idea is particularly powerful in industries with long sales cycles and limited product differentiation, such as financial services.

The purpose of identity branding is to cut through the clutter of information overload and answer the consumer's question: "Why should I do business with you?"

Identity branding is not fast or easy, but it does work. Krumroy suggests that you start by identifying up to three target markets, or identifiable groups. Each group must be broad enough to include at least two hundred people you could meet, but narrow enough that participants will see it as a separate group. The group doctors is too broad, but the group neurosurgeons is just right. Catholics is too broad, but members of St. Eulalia's parish is right on the money.

It is important to pick groups that you genuinely like, because you'll be spending a lot of time with them.

Once your groups are defined, your first goal is to meet every single person in the group. At this point, you are NOT trying to sell, simply to network. And the best way to network is to start by trying to help others, not asking them to help you.

Krumroy summarizes five basic ingredients for creating an identity brand.[137] You must:

1. Define specific markets, and decide you will own them.

2. Write a branding business plan every year, with specific objectives and measurements.

3. Include elements that prospects will perceive as memorable and high-value.

4. Provide consistent familiarity within the group.

5. Practice patience and persistence.

Identity branding is a soft-sell approach that takes significant time to pay off. But imagine how big the payoff would be if you could get in a position where whenever Chicago neurosurgeons thought of malpractice insurance, they thought of you.

Reminders

- Review the main elements of your brand on your web page. Can you identify any elements you could use more effectively in your selling?
- Display the company logo.
- Build the brand into your presentations and your elevator speech.
- Refer frequently to the best characteristics of the brand.
- Comply with corporate guidelines for using the brand message and logo.
- Consider whether identity branding would be a good strategy for you.

Ask yourself

- Can I increase sales by building more on my brand?
- Will clients recognize or respond to my brand?
- What elements of the brand will connect me to clients?
- Do prospects have a good reason to buy from me?
- If not, would identity branding increase my sales?

> *"All official institutions of language are repeating machines: school, sports, advertising, popular songs, news, all continually repeat."*
> *— Roland Barthes*

Chapter 16

Repeat the message

How pure is Ivory Soap? That's right: 99 and 44/100 percent pure. And how do you know that? Because the makers of Ivory soap have been saying that since 1882. They have repeated this message for more than twelve decades, over 120 years. They told you, they told your mother, they told your grandmother, and they told your great grandmother. Over and over and over and over.

Some of the best remembered ads in the history of advertising are the ones that were repeated the most, such as a 1950s TV ad for Anacin which illustrated a headache with a hammer banging away on an anvil.

The black and white ad started by showing an attractive young mother, with her ideal son playing quietly in the background. Mom looks like she is in pain. As she massages her head, she suddenly lashes out at the clearly innocent boy, "Can't you play someplace else?"

Johnny looks mystified and ready to dissolve in tears. Then Mom's conscience speaks out in a TV announcer's voice: "Control yourself. Sure you have a headache, but don't take it out on him." The answer is just a pill away: Anacin.

One expert described this as "probably the most hated ad of all time. It makes 'Stop squeezing the Charmin,' 'How 'bout a Hawaiian Punch,' and 'Ring around the collar,' look like playground exercises . . . .During the Cuban missile crisis, while we were biting our fingernails in nuclear-bomb anxiety, Walter Cronkite interrupted the broadcast with: 'And now a word for Anacin.'"[138]

TABLE 7

TOP 10 JINGLES OF THE 20TH CENTURY

1. You deserve a break today (McDonald's).

2. Be all that you can be (U.S. Army).

3. Pepsi Cola hits the spot (Pepsi Cola).

4. M'm, m'm good (Campbell's).

5. See the USA in your Chevrolet (GM).

6. I wish I was an Oscar Meyer Wiener (Oscar Meyer).

7. Double your pleasure, double your fun (Wrigley's Doublemint gum).

8. Winston tastes good like a cigarette should (Winston).

9. It's the real thing (Coca-Cola).

10. Brylcreem – A little dab'll do ya.

Source: Garfield, Bob. "Top 100 Advertising Campaigns of the Century." *Advertising Age.* www.adage.com/century/jingles.html

---

Even the ad agency executive behind this campaign, Rosser Reeves, described the Anacin spots as "the most hated commercials in the history of advertising." But he argued that "a hard sell advertisement, like a diesel motor, must be judged on whether it performs what it was designed to do."[139]

The ad was designed to sell Anacin, and in its first eighteen months, sales increased from $18 million to $54 million. Although the original commercial cost only $8,200 to produce, Anacin ultimately spent $85 million repeating it for the next ten years. According to one report, "Reeves was once asked by a client what his seven hundred agency people did while they kept running the same ad for a decade. He replied that they were engaged in keeping the client from changing the advertising."[140] (More about Rosser Reeves and his concept of the "Unique Selling Proposition" appeared in Chapter 4, "Add Value.")

This book helps you.

Even when repetition gets annoying, it can lead to purchase anyway. And repetition is especially memorable when set to music. Table 7 lists the top ten jingles of the century, according to *Advertising Age*. How many can you hum? If you don't know a few, it's probably because they were before your time, like the Pepsi jingle which was played 296,426 times starting in 1949.

Repetition can lead to liking. One psychologist performed a series of studies in which people were asked to rate the attractiveness of stimuli they had seen anywhere from zero to twenty-five times, including yearbook photos, Chinese characters, and nonsense words. The graph showed a nicely mathematical result: the more that a person had seen a particular stimulus, the more they liked it.[141]

Repetition can also lead to belief. Joseph Goebbels, the man behind Hitler's propaganda machine, controlled public opinion in Nazi Germany based on a simple premise: "What the masses term truth is that information which is most familiar."[142] A number of studies have also provided experimental evidence for this idea: if you hear something often enough, you start to believe that it is true.

Applying the principle

One of the first to write about the power of repetition in sales was John Patterson, who founded the National Cash Register Company in the 1880s, and built one of the first large sales forces with systematic procedures. Patterson helped develop many concepts which have since become common, including regional sales offices, sales quotas, and daily reports. And some of the most famous figures in the history of sales – including Thomas Watson[143] who went on to establish IBM's sales force – started out working for Patterson.

The first sales script was written in 1887 by Patterson's brother-in-law Joseph Crane. It listed precise instructions about what to say, when to say it, how to say it, and when to point to the cash drawer. The script was built around a tight and logical demonstration, which kept returning to repeat the central sales message.

Every sales person was required to memorize this script, and tested on their ability to repeat it, word for word, while sounding natural. If sales people were unable to master the details, or if managers found that they drifted from the precise words in actual sales calls, they were fired.[144] Those were the days!

Several of the ideas in other chapters are also related to the idea of repetition. If you invent a slogan (Chapter 14), it will have power only if you repeat it over and over. And one of the ideas behind relationship selling (see Chapter 26, Don't stop) is to keep your name and your solution in front of people as much as possible. To get the sale, you often must cross the prospect's desk on just the right day. The trick here is to do it often enough to be remembered, but not so often as to become annoying.

Reminders

- In every meeting and correspondence with your client, return to the core message.
- Tell them what you're going to say, say it, then tell them you said it.
- Make your argument memorable with anecdotes, stories, facts and figures. Then repeat the message.
- Start and end every meeting and presentation by repeating your main point.
- Find a variety of ways to restate your central sales message, without sounding too repetitious.

Ask yourself

- Do I state my main point at the beginning and end of every presentation?
- Can I state my central sales message four different ways?
- Do I need to be careful to avoid repeating too much? Yes, I do. Yes, I do.

"Who ever loved that loved not at first sight."
— Christopher Marlowe

Chapter 17

Make a good first impression

As the experts like to say, you won't get a second chance to make a first impression. And that first impression can make a big difference in your sales success.

In the marketing classic *Positioning: The Battle for Your Mind*, Al Ries and Jack Trout cite evidence that it is more important to be first than to be great. Hertz beats Avis, Goodyear beats Firestone, and McDonald's beats Burger King. On the average, the "first brand into the brain" gets double the market share of the second, which in turn gets double the market share of the third.[145]

They offer this advice to marketers: "You should build brand loyalty in a supermarket the same way you build mate loyalty in a marriage. You get there first, and then be careful not to give them a reason to switch."[146]

Psychological research has proven this power. For example, one study focused on the importance of first impressions in job interviews. One group rated candidates after a full twenty-minute job interview, another saw only a thirty-second video clip of the same meetings. Although the clip was just long enough for the candidates to say hello and sit down, the people who were limited to first impressions chose the same candidates as those who conducted full interviews.

Three major factors determined which job candidate was chosen: physical attractiveness, expressiveness, and "interaction synchrony," a kind of non-verbal dance in which people coordinate gestures and mirror each others' postures, perhaps subconsciously.

Researcher Frank Bernieri came to the radical conclusion that employers would be better off basing hiring decisions strictly on resumes and skipping job interviews entirely since "the interview is going to make you attend to irrelevant criteria."[147]

First impressions have also been shown to make a big difference in high school students' choice of a college. According to John Barry, associate director of university communications at the University of Connecticut, "Our research corroborates what national research consistently shows—that for a high percentage of prospective students, the campus tour is the single biggest influence on whether they will attend a particular college or university."

Advertisers sometimes take advantage of the power of first impressions by building positive expectations even before a product is introduced. The most famous example may be the weeks before the Beatles first came to America in 1964. Capitol Records funded a massive campaign to whip up interest. Giveaways included "Be a Beatles Booster" buttons, "The Beatles Are Coming" stickers, and a large Beatles poster with state of the art battery-powered spring-mounted heads of Paul, John, George, and Ringo. Every person on the Capitol sales staff was also given a Beatles wig and ordered to wear it throughout the business day.[148]

When the Beatles appeared on the *Ed Sullivan Show*, two nights after they landed, the success of this campaign was obvious to everyone in America. There had been sixty thousand requests for the eight hundred seats in the Ed Sullivan theatre,[149] and during the broadcast, the United States had its lowest crime rate in fifty years.[150]

Applying the principle

Communications consultant Bill Lampton offered seven tips for creating a positive impression when you meet someone new:[151]

1. Make the other person the center of the action and conversation.[152]
2. Demonstrate good listening skills by giving positive verbal cues, such as "What did you do next?"
3. Use the person's name.
4. Be careful with humor.
5. "Give up the need to be right." Don't challenge other people's opinions unless you know them well, and maybe not even then.
6. Attend to your grooming and dress. Experts suggest that you dress not for the job you have, but rather for the job you want.
7. If your natural speaking style sounds unsophisticated or uneducated, work on it. Speak clearly, be animated, and don't mumble.

Reminders

- Remember that "You won't get a second chance to make a first impression."
- Identify your key points in advance and be sure to get to them quickly.
- In a phone call, plan to get people talking quickly.
- For emails, think how the message will be perceived. If this was one of ten messages you received, could it look like spam? Personalize the subject line, and make it interesting and informative.
- Check all written communications in your spell checker and your grammar checker.
- Rehearse your voice mails.
- For face-to-face meetings, consider your shoes.
- Be early for your appointments, but not too early.

- If you are using a laptop, make sure your presentation is ready so you don't have to wait for the computer to boot up.
- Make sure that your brochure is at the top of your papers. ^ *or info kit*
- Before a first meeting, make sure you can pronounce the person's name correctly. If you are meeting Ms. Przsybysewski for the first time, verify that her name sounds like PRA SHIB A SHU SKEE.

Ask yourself

- How could I improve the subject line of an email to a prospect or the opening sentence of my next cold call letter?
- When I meet someone new, what can I do to create an immediate positive impression?
- How could I improve the impression in the first few minutes of a speech or the first seconds in a voice mail message?
- Can I explain the impression that I'm trying to make?

> *"Storytelling reveals meaning*
> *without committing the error of defining it."*
> *— Hannah Arendt*

Chapter 18

Tell a story

Which would you rather hear: a list of features and benefits for a new accounting program, or a true story about how Evelyn was able to get out a critical invoice quickly on the day that she needed to rush to the day care center? Most people would choose the story, and case studies have a long and successful history in both advertising and sales.

In the 1920s, a young copywriter named John Caples was hired to write an ad for a home-study music course. His headline still catches the eye today: "They laughed when I sat down at the piano. But when I started to play. . . ."

In the style of the 1920s, the ad was a story of several hundred words, starting at a party: "Arthur had just played 'The Rosary.' The room rang with applause. I decided this would be a dramatic moment for me to make my debut. To the amusement of all my friends I strode confidently over to the piano and sat down. 'Jack is up to his old tricks,' somebody chuckled. The crowd laughed. They were all certain I couldn't play a single note."

The drama builds for several hundred words. By the end, "the last notes of the *Moonlight Sonata* died away, the room resounded with a sudden roar of applause . . . . Men shook my hand – wildly congratulated me – pounded me on the back in their enthusiasm! Everyone was exclaiming with delight."

You too could be a hit at parties by learning to play the piano. To find out how, all you had to do was clip a coupon in the bottom right corner of the ad to get a free copy of "Music Lessons in Your Own Home," by Dr. Frank Crane.[153]

The line became so famous that it was used in vaudeville routines, and *Advertising Age* ranked this number 45 in its list of the top one hundred advertising campaigns of the century. In explaining why, they wrote: "By contemporary standards, 'They laughed when I sat down at the piano' is a transparently disingenuous dramatization of a dubious promise, yet its triumph-of-the-nebbish approach informs direct-response advertising still today . . . . 'They laughed when I sat down at the piano' may fall a bit short in the facts, but in exploring the roiling psychology of self-esteem, it overflows with human truth."[154]

Caples went on to become a famous advertising expert,[155] and the formula is still used today. In fact, the fifth edition of Caples's classic book *Tested Advertising Methods* reproduces a recent magazine ad that begins: "My husband laughed when I ordered our carpet through the mail. But when I saved fifty percent . . . ."[156]

Stories often help people to remember ads. The most memorable advertisement of 2003 featured rocker Ozzy Osbourne, who first became famous biting the heads off bats in his Black Sabbath days. The ad starts with the Osbourne children that MTV made famous – Kelly and Jack – drinking Pepsi Twist. But when they peel off their faces, it's Ozzy's worst nightmare – his kids are actually clean-cut Mormons, Donnie and Marie Osmond. According to a survey published by Advertising Age and IAG, telling a story made this the best remembered ad of the year.

Applying the principle

If you want to know how sales gurus feel about this principle, just open any of their books to a random page. You'll probably find yourself reading a story.

Soon after Zig Ziglar graduated from high school in Yazoo City, Mississippi, he went to work as a door-to-door salesman for Wearever aluminum cookware. For the first two and a half years, Zig had little success, and lived a marginal financial life from one sale to the next. "When our first baby was born," Zig reported, "I had to literally go out and sell two sets of cookware to get her out of the hospital." Then an executive pulled him aside at a regional sales meeting and told Zig that he could be "a great one" if he just learned to work in a more disciplined and efficient way. "Those words inspired me to become the number two salesman in a company of seven thousand in one year."[157]

In 1955 Zig began teaching sales techniques at the Dale Carnegie Institute. He went on to found Ziglar Training Systems, and since 1970 Zig has traveled over five million miles giving public speeches about his sales techniques and philosophy of life. If you ever attended one, you heard a lot of stories.

If you are the type of person who entertains friends and family with amusing anecdotes about the time your car broke down in Tuscaloosa, you are undoubtedly already selling with stories.

But even if you're not a natural, this is a skill most people can develop quickly with relatively little practice. You just have to define your sales message, figure out what recent events can illustrate your point, look for the details that will make the story engaging, then practice, practice, practice.

Note how the Zig Ziglar examples above include many specific details including the number of sets of cookware he had to sell to re-claim his first child (two), the number of people who worked for Wearever when he shot to the top (seven thousand) and the number of miles he's traveled since 1970 (over five million).

For example, suppose you are a broker advising on retirement portfolios, and you want to emphasize the importance of patience and diversification. With a little research, you can easily find a true story about someone who ignored this advice when the market peaked in 2001, and had a 401K plan which included nothing but dotcoms. Build the story around details: what was the value of his favorite stock before the crash and after? When was he hoping to retire when his portfolio was at its peak, and what does he expect now?

Reminders

- Whenever you give a presentation, tell at least one story. *and one funny story*
 - Consider adding mini-stories to some emails and letters.
- Plan how to use personal anecdotes to support your central sales message.
- Collect stories of satisfied clients, and how you met their needs.
- While the best stories are likely to be based on your personal experience, you can use stories from others, as long as you are completely open and honest about the source.
- Follow these steps to create a memorable sales story:
  - Define the sales message.
  - Pick an interesting event.
  - Dramatize with true details.
  - Practice, practice, practice.

Ask yourself

- What's happened to me in the last month that I could turn into a sales story?

- What sales message should I support with a story?
- What clients or friends had experiences related to this sales message?
- Do other members of my sales team have compelling stories that I might adopt?
- Does my story have enough details to be dramatic and memorable?

"Drama is life with the dull bits cut out."
— Alfred Hitchcock

Chapter 19

Dramatize the dull

It's hard to be duller than a white dress shirt. In the 1950s, business dress shirts were acceptable in any color, as long as they were white. A banker would never think of making a loan to a man who wore stripes or French blue. Because all white dress shirts are pretty much alike, the advertisers who sold them had little to work with. How much can you say about the buttons or the pocket?

In one of the most famous campaigns in the history of advertising, David Ogilvy dramatized the dull with "the man in the Hathaway shirt." The original Hathaway man was a friend of Ogilvy's named Baron George Wrangell and the key to his success was the ever so mysterious eye patch. There are conflicting versions of who came up with the idea,[158] but there is no doubt that the campaign propelled Hathaway from obscurity since 1837 to fame and fortune for the forty years that these ads ran in *The New Yorker.*

The Hathaway man was everything *New Yorker* readers wanted to be: sophisticated, distinguished, brilliant, athletic, kind to small animals and irresistible to the opposite sex. In advertisements running over several decades, "we saw the Baron conducting the New York Philharmonic at Carnegie Hall, copying a Goya at the Met, driving a tractor, fencing, sailing, dealing for a Renoir, all the time looking as if he were thinking about the upcoming cocktail hour." And soon after you started reading about the Baron's latest escapade, you were immersed in details of Hathaway shirts' "impeccable taste" where "even the stitching has an ante-bellum elegance about it."[159]

Research supports the value of vivid examples and drama.

From 1951 to 1990, the Baron moved from adventure to adventure, and Hathaway sold shirts. But all good things must come to an end, and the eye patch man was ultimately replaced by a smirking fellow who needed a shave. Perhaps the world was no longer subtle enough for a shirt identified by a red "H" embroidered into the tail, where no one could see it.

These days, successful shirt brands require you to wear their logos on your chest. That way, every human being you pass in the street will know that you are so successful that you can afford to pay for the shirt with the polo pony. The principle of dramatizing the dull is the same, but the execution has been adapted to contemporary tastes.

Another way to dramatize dull product differences is by creating a contest that pits them against each other, as in the Pepsi Challenge campaign of the late 1970s. Pepsi set up stands in grocery store parking lots and asked shoppers to taste test glasses of Pepsi vs. Coke. Pepsi consistently won by a convincing margin, and inexpensive ads showed one person after another explaining why they preferred Pepsi. As a result, in 1979 Pepsi passed Coke in grocery store sales for the first time ever, after several decades of trying.[160]

Psychological research also supports the value of using vivid examples and dramatization. Vivid examples attract attention, cut through the clutter of information overload, and are more likely to be remembered.

One study of this phenomenon was done in the late 1970s, when the government began offering homeowners free energy audits, to make them more energy efficient by insulating houses.[161] The government found it was easy to get people to sign up for a free audit, but much harder to get them to act on the results.

Researchers compared two ways of presenting the same information. In a "matter of fact" presentation, they informed the homeowner that cracks around doors let in cold air, and weather stripping could save money. In the vivid presentation, they dramatized this dull fact: "If you were to add up all the cracks around . . . these doors, you'd have a hole . . . the circumference of a basketball. Suppose someone poked a hole the size of a basketball in your living room wall. Think . . . about all the heat you'd be losing."

Only about fifteen percent of the people who heard the simple factual presentation went out and bought weather stripping. But the vivid presentation led sixty-one percent to action, an advantage of about four to one.[162]

Another study looked at the effect of vivid examples on mock jurors in an experimental simulation of a murder trial.[163] One group heard just the facts, while a second was given vivid emotional information, including the fact that the murder victim was an honors student, and her younger sister now had trouble sleeping through the night. While this vivid information was legally irrelevant, it led jurors to recommend harsher punishment.

Applying the principle

Marketers often use this principle to make dry facts memorable. When the Queen Mary 2 was launched, the company website noted that it was "the world's largest, longest, tallest, grandest ocean liner ever." Few people would ever remember that it was 1,132 feet long, but they may well have remembered the company's dramatic comparison: if the Empire State Building were laid on its side, the Queen Mary 2 would be almost as long.[164]

The concept of "dramatizing the dull" can often be combined with "tell a story" to make your sales message more memorable. Consider the problem of selling business insurance to restaurant owners. Insurance is one of those things that nobody wants to think about, partly because the details of policy coverage can put some people to sleep.

For example, one agent we worked with often told stories about when he owned restaurants, including the time the hot water pipe burst and ruined his walls, ceiling and carpet. His agent came by soon after and said, don't worry about a thing, we'll take care of it.

When the reimbursement check arrived six weeks later, it was fifty-four hundred dollars short of what he had expected. That's when he read the contract more carefully and found that his property coverage was for actual cash value, not replacement value. His carpet had cost nine thousand dollars three years before. The insurer depreciated the carpet on a five-year schedule, leaving forty percent of the value, or thirty-six hundred dollars.

This is a great sales story on several levels. It adds a little drama to make people care more about the details of property coverage. By telling a story about a restaurant he had owned, the agent also managed to establish instant credibility and rapport with potential clients.

Reminders

- Come up with vivid analogies to make facts concrete and interesting.
- Use specific details – who, what, when, where – to make dry information more compelling.
- Start with a hook – a fact, story, or example to grab interest.

- Speak with conviction, alter your pace, and use strong gestures to reinforce your argument.

Ask yourself

- What could I do to dramatize the dull?
- How could I make key benefits sound more interesting?
- How could I make my central sales message more memorable?

"Language is the mother of thought,
not its handmaiden."
– Karl Kraus

Chapter 20

Write powerful headlines

Do you think people would respond differently to these
two headlines:

- Are you afraid of making mistakes in English?

- Do you make these mistakes in English?

Caples reported that when a mail order advertiser tried
both, one headline was a success and the other a
failure.[165] Can you guess which and why?

The second headline is the one that worked, and Caples
says the key is the word "these," with its promise of free
information and specific advice. It appeals to curiosity for
everyone, and to self-interest for anyone worried about
their ability to communicate. It may also offer a certain
self-satisfied amusement, if you are certain that only
others would make silly mistakes.

In the 1920s, the Phoenix Home Life Insurance Company
built a highly successful business based almost entirely
on effective headlines – direct mail ads which were
constantly improved by research.[166] Among their most
effective headlines:

- Advice to wives whose husbands don't save money.

- A vacation that lasts the rest of your life.

- How to make two investments with one dollar.

- Here's one question you shouldn't ask your wife.

Note that none of these headlines mention the word insurance, which is what they were selling. That's because their research found that the word "insurance" makes readers' eyes glaze over. But when the same concepts are covered under the headline "financial plan," most people will keep reading and many will respond.

My personal favorite headline appeared on a circular for a mid-nineteenth century law firm and consisted of a single word:

Money

The details appeared beneath the headline: "Plenty of money for soldiers and soldiers' heirs . . . . More liberal laws. Less proof required." The ads explained that by law, any soldier who served at least thirty days between 1832 and 1842 in the Black Hawk War or Cherokee War was entitled to eight dollars per month. You could get fifty dollars per month if you proved that you "require an attendant much of the time" or seventy-two dollars per month for proving that you "require an attendant all of the time." For a fee, the enterprising law firm H. J. Hayden would do the paperwork and get you the money. If you wanted to know the fee, you'd have to go see them.

Since people are five times more likely to read a headline than an ad,[167] experienced copywriters focus much of their energy on writing powerful headlines, and then testing them.

Applying the principle

You probably don't write headlines for articles or ads. But you do write emails, and you know from your own experience that you will often fail to read an email if the subject line fails to grab you. And you do write letters, where a strong first line can play the same role.

So how can you write better headlines? You can see the fifth edition of John Caples's *Tested Advertising Methods* for over 250 pages of advice. Or you can just start with the list below, derived from Caples's book:

- Use words that grab attention.
- Use words that provoke curiosity.
- Ask a question.
- Cite facts and figures.
- Be positive.
- Go beyond curiosity.
- Limit to three words or less.
- Make it sound like news.
- Include the date.
- Provide useful information.
- Tell a story.
- Cite a testimonial.
- Offer a survey or test.
- Use "reverse psychology;" for example, five reasons you should *not* buy my product.
- If price is critical to your sale, include the price, announce a sale, or highlight easy payment terms.
- Keep headlines believable.
- Appeal to self-interest.
- Test your headlines over and over.

In his book *Selling to VITO,* Anthony Parinello explains how headlines can be especially important in selling to "Very Important Top Officers, or VITOs." He notes that "Research shows that, on average, people decide within about eight seconds whether or not to continue reading an unexpected piece of mail."[168] Since important people may spend even less time, he suggests that prospecting letters to VITOs begin with a headline, and he offers a detailed plan for tying your product to their need to maximize the headline's effectiveness.

Reminders

- Use headline techniques that have been proven in advertising.

- Use words that grab attention, such as: quick, easy, new, now, introducing, announcing, at last, this, wanted, advice, because, if.
- Use words that provoke curiosity, such as: how to, how, why, which, who else.
- Keep headlines believable.
- Write a headline for your next letter and work on it each day for a week.
- Start with a statement that establishes your credibility, including factual info or exact quotes.
- Always remember the most critical piece of advice from John Caples' book *Tested Advertising Methods:* "Keep hammering at the reader with –you –you – you."[169]

Ask yourself

- Does the subject line of my email provoke interest, or does it sound like spam?
- Should I include a catchy, dramatic headline in my next letter?
- Is my headline tied to my objectives?
- Have I tested my headline?
- Do I appeal to self-interest with benefits rather than features?

"The secret of being a bore is to tell everything."
– Voltaire

Chapter 21

Less is more

Many companies have applied the idea of less is more to keep their sales pitch clear and concise. The best example is Maytag. Why is the Maytag repairman lonely? That's right, he has nothing to do because Maytag appliances are so dependable that they never break down.[170]

The marketplace for appliances is huge. A few years ago, Maytag estimated that every day Americans wash fifty-six million loads of dishes and seventy-seven million loads of laundry.[171]

Before Maytag's "Ol' Lonely" campaign started in 1967, appliance ads usually emphasized new features: this model uses less water, that model has more cycles. In the first TV ad introducing the "Ol' Lonely" character, a trainer taught new Maytag repairmen how to fill the long hours between service calls with knitting and crossword puzzles. In another, Maytag bragged, "We do less all day than most people do before sunrise."

Over one hundred different Maytag ads have been run about Ol' Lonely. The campaign has gone on for so long that the first two actors who played Ol' Lonely's died and had to be replaced.[172] My favorite Maytag commercial took "less is more" to its logical extreme by having no action and no dialog at all. The entire commercial showed a Maytag repairman and his basset hound snoring, while his tools sat nearby unused, and the clock ticked loudly.

The dependability theme has also been stressed in Maytag print ads built on client testimonials, like the nun who washed fifteen loads of habits and curtains every week.

In 1993, Maytag celebrated the company's one hundredth birthday by running a contest to find the oldest Maytag washing machine still in use. Entries were mailed to company headquarters at One Dependability Square in Newton, Iowa. This "less is more" campaign has been spectacularly successful in establishing Maytag's reputation as "the dependability people" and in increasing sales.[173]

Kodak's first cameras were successful because they kept it simple.

Closely related to "less is more" is the phrase "keep it simple, stupid," often shortened to KISS. The phrase harkens back to a more innocent time when you could call someone "stupid" as a sign of rough affection, without risk of being sued by someone who was, dare we say, smartness challenged.

Kodak built an entire industry on KISS. Before Kodak, photographers had to travel with portable darkrooms to develop bulky glass plates. Then, in 1888, George Eastman introduced a new Kodak camera for anyone who wanted to take photos without touching darkroom chemicals.

Eastman hired a professional to write the copy for the first instruction manual and ads, then fired him when he failed to keep it simple enough. Eastman coined the first advertising slogan himself: "You press the button, we do the rest."[174] The first ad went on to explain that this was "the only camera that anybody can use without instruction."

With Kodak's first camera, you took a few hundred photos then mailed the entire camera to 343 State Street, Rochester, NY. Kodak developed the prints, loaded your camera with new film, and mailed it all back.[175] The original mail-in camera was so successful that the company could not keep up with demand. New York newspapers wrote editorials complaining about the delay in getting their pictures back.[176]

In December 1891, the good became even better: Kodak introduced the ABC camera which allowed you to remove the film yourself. In broad daylight! Demand skyrocketed again, and Kodak had to slow down the sales effort while they built capacity.[177]

The fad was sudden and pervasive. Characters known as "beach fiends" became known for prowling resorts to take photos of women in their bathing suits. At least one resort posted a sign stating, "People are forbidden to use their Kodaks on the beach."

Kodak's advertising slogan was even immortalized in a song from Gilbert and Sullivan's operetta *Utopia*:

> The Kodaks do their best:
> If evidence you would possess
> Of what is maiden bashfulness
> You need a button press—
> And we do the rest!

The Kodak company went on to create a new industry for amateur photography and dominated it for over a century. All because they kept it simple.

It is easy to forget that less is more, and to waste an enormous amount of time on tasks that don't matter.

And it's a constant struggle to figure out how much is good enough. Management experts often talk about the "80/20 rule":[178] eighty percent of the work is accomplished in the first twenty percent of the time.

That's one reason so many deadlines are missed. People finish the easy eighty percent quickly, and assume that the rest will go just as fast. But it never does: that last twenty percent of the work will take eighty percent of your time.

That's why managers urge employees to "pick the right moment to be perfect." If you're a brain surgeon, that's all the time. But for the rest of us, a rough draft or first approximation is often enough to meet an immediate need.

In business, time is money, and sometimes the best course is to save time and money by stopping before you have achieved the best. As the Tao philosopher Lin Yutang put it: "Besides the noble art of getting things done, there is the noble art of leaving things undone. The wisdom of life consists in the elimination of non-essentials."

Applying the principle

The "elevator speech" is a perfect example of the less is more principle. The concept originated in venture capital circles, based on the idea that a struggling entrepreneur happened to walk into an elevator with Donald Trump and wanted to make a pitch before the Donald reached his floor.

Can you summarize your core message in five seconds? Can you do it in a minute? Do you have a few elevator speeches ready for different audiences and different situations? You'll have to decide the details that best fit your product and your market, but here are some of the elements to consider:

- *Length.* Pick the shortest length you can, and stick with it.

- *KISS.* Keeping it simple is especially important when you're riding an elevator. Test the message on your friends, and keep changing it until everyone gets your message.

- *Use a hook.* Reporters are taught to begin every news article with a "hook" to pique the reader's interest and attract attention. That can be a great way to start an elevator speech, as long as you have enough time.

- *Fit in.* Your opening or your hook must feel natural in your environment. If you start an elevator ride by saying "Hi. I'm a motivational speaker," you are indeed getting right to the point, but will probably succeed mostly in getting listeners to hit the button and get off at an earlier floor.

- *Show your passion.* Your customers want to buy from someone who has energy and enthusiasm. Just beware of crossing the boundary into hokeyness.

- *Leave them asking for more.* You are not going to close a sale in fifteen to sixty seconds. You are trying to get people to return for a longer conversation. End your mini-speech with a call to action such as a request for a business card or more.

- *Practice, practice, practice.* After you think your message is perfect, start practicing until it gets much, much better.

Elevator speeches will be especially useful at networking events and conferences, but must always be adapted so that they sound natural and fresh.

Reminders

- The more you say, the less your audience will hear.
- You cannot bore someone into buying your product.
- Position your product as the simple solution that will do exactly what your client needs, and ignore everything else.
- Keep your sentences short. (The single most important factor in comprehension is sentence length.)

- When you write a letter to a new prospect, limit it to a single page, and lead to a simple conclusion, for example, "I will call you next Friday."
- Define a simple core message for every email, every phone call, and every meeting.
- Make sure that core message gets across.
- When closing, watch for buying signs including verbal agreement, asking for concrete information, smiling, leaning forward, and non-verbal cues of agreement. Then go for the close.
- If your pipeline is full, push to win early or lose early, and recognize negative buying signs:
  - Delayed decisions.
  - Failure to get return calls.
  - "It won't be necessary to meet my boss."
  - Sales requirements that change suddenly.
- Prepare several elevator speeches that summarize your core message in five to sixty seconds, for different settings.
- Test and improve your elevator speeches.

Ask yourself

- What is my most important and most central message?
- What's the minimum time I need to present this

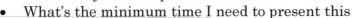

message?
on at an appropriate level

dvantage early and often?
stomers give me eighty
w much of my attention do

"When we are happy we are always good,
but when we are good we are not always happy."
— Oscar Wilde

Chapter 22

Make people happy

Many ads include the message: buy my product, and you
will be happy.

Häagen-Dazs was the first ice cream to make this explicit
by running ads which emphasize pleasure. When the
brand was launched in the 1950s, most ice cream
companies competed on cost. Häagen-Dazs went in a
different direction by creating a luxury ice cream with
expensive flavorings, more butterfat, and less air.

Reuben Mattus created the high-end marketing, built
around the ice cream's mythical origins in Denmark. He
placed an umlaut over the ä to contribute to the exotic
image, despite the fact that umlauts are not used in
Danish. In fact, Häagen-Dazs was started in the Bronx.
Mattus explained it this way: "I figured there were
people who hated the Irish, there were people who hated
the Italians, there were people who hated the Jews. But
nobody hated the Danes."[179]

Campaigns consistently stressed that Häagen-Dazs will
make you happy. One of the most famous, in the 1990s,
showed a couple preparing for bed. A woman is shown
lounging in her nightgown, while the gentleman walks
upstairs wearing boxer shorts and a smile. The voice-
over said: "At 11:30 at night, there's one thing better
than sleep or television or flannel pajamas or even
flossing." The camera pans to the man's hands with a

pint of Häagen-Dazs and two spoons for the tag-line: "Häagen-Dazs. It's better than anything."[180]

Ads offering PG-rated happiness are even more common. In 1978, when Pepsi supermarket sales were higher than Coke's for the first time in history, Coke responded with the "Have a Coke and a Smile" campaign. The most famous ad started with Pittsburgh Steeler Mean Joe Greene[181] limping off the field.[182] An awfully cute young boy holds out a sixteen-ounce Coke saying shyly, "Mr. Greene. Mr. Greene." The defensive end turns and snarls, "Yeah?" "I just want you to know I think, I think you're the best ever," stammers the kid. "Yeah, sure," says Greene as he turns away.

In desperation, the kid holds out his Coke. Greene declines at first. Then he takes the Coke, and drains all sixteen ounces in one football-player sized chug. The music starts for "Have a Coke and a Smile." As the dejected boy turns away, Greene says, "Hey, kid," and throws him his jersey. The music rises in the background, and everybody is happy.[183]

In 2001, when *USA Today* conducted an online poll of the greatest Super Bowl ads of all time ("Super Bowl's greatest"), the Mean Joe Greene commercial ranked number one.

If you want to be happy, and think psychology might help, read Martin Seligman's book, *Authentic Happiness: Using the New Positive Psychology to Realize Your Potential for Lasting Fulfillment.*[184] The book explains dozens of fascinating studies, organized around this formula: H (enduring level of happiness) = S (set range) + C (circumstances of your life) + V (voluntary factors).

The "set range" refers to your "happiness thermostat" which pulls you back to a constant level. My favorite study followed the fortunes of twenty-two lottery winners.[185] After they stopped jumping up and down in joy, the lucky ticket holders gradually went back to baseline levels, and ended up about as happy as twenty-two matched controls. The same study also looked at

spinal cord accident victims, and found that within a few
years they too were about as happy as the control group.
These are examples of the "hedonic treadmill." People
adjust to most things rather quickly, both good and bad,
then return to their steady state of happiness.

Happiness only recently became a topic for psychological research.

Happiness is only about half environmental; the other
half was inherited from mom and pop. As Seligman puts
it, "roughly fifty percent of almost every personality trait
turns out to be attributable to genetic inheritance."[186]

Most of us overestimate the importance of C, life
circumstances. In fact, money makes little difference
"once you are comfortable enough to buy this book."[187]
Research suggests that moving to Florida or getting an
advanced degree won't help either. Even objective health
is surprisingly unrelated to happiness, although your
subjective view of your health does make a difference.

Biswas-Diener interviewed thirty-one pavement dwellers
and thirty-two prostitutes in Calcutta, India. Yes, they
wanted more money. But they reported a surprising
degree of life satisfaction in such areas as morality, food,
family, and friends. Seligman describes surveys of life
satisfaction with over one thousand people from forty
nations. The United States scored lower in life
satisfaction than the Netherlands, Ireland, Canada,
Denmark, and Switzerland, all countries with less
purchasing power. And US citizens are only a little more
satisfied than those in the People's Republic of China,
who had just a small fraction of US purchasing power.[188]

About half of Seligman's book is devoted to ways you can
become happier through voluntary factors, such as
changing the way you look at the past, developing the
Buddhist concept of mindfulness, and understanding and
building on your "signature strengths" such as humor,

perseverance, integrity, generosity, optimism, and spirituality. To diagnose yours, take the test at his web page: www.authentichappiness.org.

If you are determined to try to increase happiness through life factors, get married, become religious, and find a lot of friends. People who have a network of close personal relationships are less likely to get sick and more likely to live long lives. And when people are asked what they need to be happy or what makes their lives meaningful, the first thing they mention is relationships with family and friends. As C.S. Lewis put it, "The sun looks down on nothing half so good as a household laughing together over a meal."

For more practical advice, see another Seligman book: *Learned Optimism: How to Change Your Mind and Your Life.*[189]

You probably shouldn't try to create lifelong personal relationships in your next sales call, but you can try to make them just a little bit happy.

Applying the principle

The very best way to make people happy in sales is to sell them things they need, priced reasonably, described honestly, and backed by your personal commitment.

Discounts make people happy too, but the bean counters like it better if you don't cut prices.

List of free ezine articles & how to access them

Free stuff can increase happiness too. Many people believe in the selling power of free ball point pens and Post-it notes, which you can easily purchase on the web for remarkably low prices.[190] Experts say that the best giveaways will be things that are high value to your customer and low cost to you.[191]

If you run out of ideas, give chocolate. But don't be cheap. Buy the best brand of chocolate that will appeal to your customers. If you lean more toward licorice, I feel sorry for you. Recognize that you are part of a disadvantaged minority, and buy chocolate.

Unfortunately, any discussion of making people happy must also admit that some of the time, some of the customers will not be entirely one hundred percent thrilled. It doesn't matter whose fault it is, your job is to make them happier. Try to:

• Give customers an opportunity to vent.

• Stay calm.

• Apologize.

• Prove that you are listening.

• Thank them for the information.

• Do everything you can to solve the problem.

You should be happy too. You deserve it. Besides, research suggests that your happiness will be linked to productivity, if you do it the right way.

When the Gallup organization surveyed over two hundred fifty thousand sales people, they concluded that the single most important factor in both job satisfaction and performance is the fit between your personality and your job. The book *Discover Your Sales Strengths* offers help in both assessing your strengths, and improving fit, which is "the fastest, surest, and most dramatic way to improve your success and your job satisfaction."[192]

The most important tip is that you must find a way to change the job to fit you. If you try to change yourself to fit the job, it won't work.

All right, that's enough about you. If only one person is going to be happy, let's make it the customer.

Reminders

- Be honest, sell people only what they need, price it reasonably, and back it with your personal commitment.
- Make people feel good about themselves.
- Give discounts.
- Give free stuff.
- If people get angry, give them time to vent, then try to bring them around to considering solutions.
- Follow these guidelines, from John Patterson's nineteenth century sales guides for National Cash Register[193]:
  1. Never argue.
  2. Never offend.
  3. Never think or act like you are defeated.
  4. Try to make a friend at all costs.
  5. Try to get on the same side of the fence (harmonize).

Ask yourself

- When was the last time I made a client unhappy (e.g., by showing up late for an appointment)?
- What have I done lately to make customers happy?
- Could I be happier and more productive by adapting my job to better fit my personality strengths?
- What can I do to make the sales process more fun?

"It seems odd that a man laughs so hard at his own jokes.
People think you are a bit odd, or perhaps choking."
— Mark Salzman

Chapter 23

Be cautious with humor

If you are unfunny in the comfort of your own home, the
biggest risk is that your teenagers will mock you. Which
is really a small risk, since they are going to mock you
anyway. But in an advertisement or a sales call, the
wrong kind of humor can annoy people, and damage your
image and your credibility.

Consider "Joe Isuzu," the fictional spokesperson for
American Isuzu Motors in the late 1980s.[194] To his fans,
this fast talking car salesman was not only an attention
grabber, he was a symbol that Isuzu Motors was so
confident that they could make fun of their own brand.

In a typical commercial, Joe promised that a 4x4 Isuzu
Trooper was so roomy that it could fit a symphony
orchestra or "hold every book in the Library of Congress
and if I'm lying, may lightning hit my mother." Which, of
course, it did. The commercial ended with the little old
lady going up in a poof of smoke.

Joe Isuzu did become famous as a symbol of liars
everywhere when President Ronald Reagan compared
Nicaraguan leader Daniel Ortega to "that fellow from
Isuzu." Is that the image you'd want associated with your
car company?

Humorous campaigns have sometimes proceeded even in
the face of negative reactions. The "Frito Bandito"

campaign in the late 60s was built around a cartoon character that is impossible to imagine today, complete with two six guns, a long mustache, a sombrero, and a caricature of a Mexican accent.   In 1969, when the whole world was preparing for the astronauts to land on the moon, a thirty-second TV commercial showed them being greeted by the Frito Bandito: "I ham the moon parking lot attendant. Now if you will kindly deposit one bag of cronchy Fritos corn cheeps for the first hour . . . ."[195]

In our age of political correctness, humor is riskier than ever.

The commercials were attacked for stereotyping by groups ranging from the Mexican-American Anti-Defamation Committee to Mexican Americans in Gainful Endeavor. But the commercials were selling corn chips, and Foote, Cone & Belding, the agency that created the ads, did not want to end the campaign. They tried to tone them down with four new guidelines for the animations: "1. Less grimacing. 2. No beard or gold tooth. 3. Change in facial features to guile rather than leer. 4. Friendly face and voice."[196] The changes were not enough, and in the face of congressional and media pressure, in 1971, PepsiCo reluctantly killed off the Frito Bandito.

In our age of political correctness, humor can be riskier than ever. *Backpacker* magazine faced criticism in 2000 for running an ad for Nike All Conditions Gear Air Dri-Goat trail running shoe. The ad described "the totally cool, ultra-hardcore sport of extreme trail running." With other shoes, you might run into a tree and become "a drooling, misshapen, non-extreme-trail-running husk of my former self, forced to roam the earth in a motorized wheelchair with my name embossed on one of those cute little license plates you get at carnivals or state fairs, fastened to the back." People in motorized wheelchairs were not amused, and the ad was withdrawn.

But here's what makes it so hard to ignore humor: when humor works, it can be extraordinarily effective in grabbing attention. The Super Bowl has become almost as famous for the commercials as for the football. In fact, according to a survey reported in *USA Today*, "fourteen percent of those viewing the Super Bowl will be watching just for the ads."[197]

USA Today also runs an annual focus group in which over a hundred people rate each ad as they watch. Year after year, it seems that the key to ad-meter popularity is, "Keep 'em laughing." However, whether or not those funny ads sell products is an open question.

Applying the principle

Did you hear about the agnostic, dyslexic insomniac? He stayed up all night wondering if there was a dog.

That joke came in my email, part of the never-ending procession of web humor that clutters my inbox. It's a good illustration of the key problem with humor: what's funny to me may offend you. What if I had tossed and turned all night and was not in the mood for joking about sleep? Or I think it's not nice to make fun of dyslexics? Or that agnostics deserve more respect?

We've met many sales people who use jokes as ice breakers. If it works for you, that's great, skip the rest of this chapter. But we've also heard stories about humor that did not work, such as the broker who told a joke making fun of a competitor, tried it out on one prospect, and never heard from him again. A coincidence? All right, it probably was. But maybe it proved my point. There's no way to know.

We do know that it's almost impossible to find a joke that offends no one, and that offending people is not a good way to build momentum in a sales call. So you usually have more to lose than to gain from humor. So do as I say, not as I do: be cautious with humor.

Reminders

- Carefully review every planned use of humor.
- If you think that an attempt at humor might possibly offend someone, it probably will.
- If in doubt, leave it out.

Ask yourself

- Am I a little funny?
- If not, should I avoid humor?
- What are the chances that my joke will be perceived as unfunny?
- What are the chances that my joke will offend?

> *"Round up the usual suspects."*
> *– Captain Renault in the film* Casablanca

Chapter 24

Require immediate action

The stress for immediate action is so universal, and so hard to resist, that many states have passed "cooling off" laws to protect consumers by allowing them to back out of commitments on vacation timeshares and other products within seventy-two hours of signing an agreement.

Have you ever sent away for a free pamphlet on "Planning for Retirement"? Maybe you were afraid that the company who sent it to you would soon be sending junk mail. But you did it anyway, because the pamphlet contained valuable information.

From the advertiser's point of view, your agreement to accept something free broke the ice. The first step is always the hardest, and so "foot in the door" selling techniques aim for quick agreement to something small, paving the way for later agreements to something big.

One study of the foot in the door technique asked California homeowners to allow a "Drive Carefully" sign on their front lawns. As always, there were two groups. The control group members were simply asked for their participation, and seventeen percent agreed to display the sign. For the "foot in the door group," another researcher had come to their homes two weeks earlier to ask for a much smaller step, putting a three-inch sign in the window that said "Be a Safe Driver." Almost everybody had agreed to this innocuous request. For this group, the willingness to put up the large sign on the lawn rose to seventy-six percent. The foot in the door had worked.

In another study of a phone survey in Bloomington, Indiana, people were first asked to predict what they would say if the American Cancer Society asked for three hours of help collecting donations. A few days later, someone else called to actually ask them to help collect. The ones who had predicted they would say yes agreed to collect far more often, and this simple procedure increased volunteering by seven hundred percent.[198]

> ## *The foot in the door technique has been proven in research.*

The effects can be so powerful that one of the leading experts in the field, Robert Cialdini, wrote that the foot in the door effect "scares me enough that I am rarely willing to sign a petition anymore, even for a position I support." The signed petition is the foot in the door and "has the potential to influence not only my future behavior but also my self-image in ways I may not want."[199]

Cialdini also believes that self-selling is the key to contests asking you to describe why you love a product in one hundred words or less.[200] After you write the argument, you may come to believe it yourself. That's why Amway encourages their representatives to write their sales goals down, he believes. Once you have committed yourself in writing, you are likely to work harder to achieve the goal.

Applying the principle

In *SPIN Selling,* Neil Rackham emphasizes that "successful sellers never push the customer beyond achievable limits."[201] SPIN sellers measure the success of a call not just by closes, but by "advances." Of course the close is the ultimate goal and the final definition of success, but it may happen in a small percentage of your calls, and everyone needs a reliable way to measure the success of all the others.

He defines an advance as any customer action "either in the call or after it, that moves the sale forward toward a decision."[202] His examples include:

- An agreement to attend an off-site demo.

- Help or clearance in getting you to meet a higher level of decision maker.

- An agreement to participate in a free trial of your product.

Note that all three involve the customer actually doing something, rather than just saying something. The art of selling includes the sub-art of figuring out just what kind of advance is possible, and then getting it.

When Stephan Schiffman wrote a book entitled *25 Sales Strategies That Will Boost Your Sales Today,*[203] Chapter 15 was named: "Always try to move the sale to the next step." In the most extreme example, Schiffman says that you should end every face-to-face meeting with a request for another meeting. You'll have to decide for yourself whether that's appropriate for your business. But his general advice is well taken. "Remember, the objective of the first step is to get to the next step, and that's all you want to do in each and every case."[204]

But asking for immediate action remains an art, not a science. In large accounts where the stakes are high and sales cycles are long, an entire sales meeting may be devoted to brainstorming the best next steps with a slow-moving client.

When experienced sales people can't get a big and profitable order, they may sometimes try for a small and unprofitable one. As an article in *American Salesman* put it: "When a person has signed an order for your merchandise, even though the profit is so small that it hardly compensates for the time and effort of making the call, he is no longer a prospect, he is a customer."[205]

Reminders

- Start every sales call by identifying the advance you want – a small step of progress toward the sale.
- If your attempts to make advances are consistently unsuccessful, you are probably never going to get to a sale. Move on.
- Require immediate action for yourself.
- Create a sense of urgency.
- When you near the close, give people a reason to buy now, such as a discount or a delivery schedule.
- Ask for the order.

Ask yourself

- What small customer action will help me to advance this sale?
- How could I follow up to move the sale forward?
- When the close gets near, do I hesitate to ask for the sale?

> *"I'm tired of all this nonsense about*
> *beauty being only skin-deep. That's deep enough.*
> *What do you want, an adorable pancreas?"*
> *– Jean Kerr*

Chapter **25**

Look good

How many people will read this book, and how many will form an impression from the cover?

If you went to junior high, you know that looks matter. Psychologists have proven what you and I learned by seventh grade: there is a huge bias in favor of physically attractive people. The beautiful are perceived as happier, more successful, and having better personalities, while less attractive people are judged as less disciplined and more self-indulgent.[206]

Ad photographers go to great lengths to make their products look great. When Burger King filmed the Whopper for its TV commercials: "To create an ideal bun, extra sesame seeds were pasted on with tweezers and egg white. Water was squirted on the tomatoes to give them a 'dewy fresh look' and the condiments were dabbed on meticulously with Q-tips."[207]

In the world of marketing, looks matter not just for the product itself, but also for the package it comes in. In a survey of 985 consumers, forty-six percent reported that they had discarded or returned a product in the last twelve months due to defective packaging. And nineteen percent of these packaging problems led consumers to refuse to buy that brand again.[208]

Even the color of the package can have a major impact on consumer behavior. In its early years, Microsoft's packaging used lots of forest green. But color experts noted that particular shade of green "connotes frozen vegetables and chewing gum, not high tech." Microsoft switched to crimson red and royal blue, and the rest is history.[209]

Some brands owe their success to packaging.

The color of soda cans has been linked to the tastes that consumers report: a blue background on the can gave root beer a more old-fashioned taste than a beige background. And Canada Dry's green and white can for the diet ginger ale is said to have increased sales by twenty-five percent compared to the previous red can. That's why Diet Coke designers created more than a hundred and fifty can designs before choosing the tasteful grey pinstripe.

Absolut Vodka has built a very successful brand almost entirely around attractive packaging and image.

Absolut's official marketing material explains the product's superiority:[210] "All water used in Absolut comes from its own deep well; the water's consistently even quality makes it the ideal water for a premium vodka." But for less discriminating folks like myself,[211] vodka is just a colorless liquid that gets mixed with fruit juices and makes you happy. It is the packaging and advertising that makes the difference.

The Absolut brand was founded in 1879 by Lars Olsson Smith: "Successful businessman at ten and entrepreneur at fourteen, he controlled one third of all the vodka in Sweden while he was still learning to shave."[212] Known as "The King of Vodka," he became "one of the richest men in the country, a fortune he would lose, regain and lose again. When he died in 1913, he was penniless, leaving behind him nothing but debts, angry letters and lawsuits."

In 1979, to celebrate the vodka's hundredth anniversary, Absolut's visionary president Lars Lindmark launched a campaign to export the brand. They decided on a very simple approach: every ad consisted simply of an artistic image of an Absolut bottle plus a two to three word caption such as "Absolut Perfection."

The connection of these ads to art was reinforced in 1985 when the vodka company commissioned a painting by Andy Warhol. There was only one constraint: it must feature the Absolut bottle. The result – Absolut Warhol – was the first of four hundred commissions, many of which have appeared in ads. Series included Absolut Expressions by fourteen African-American artists, Absolut Latino by sixteen artists from Central and South America, and Absolut Glasnost from twenty-six Soviet artists. Absolut Art includes paintings, sculptures, quilts, and even "agro-art": a Kansas wheat farm the size of twelve football fields sown in the shape of an Absolut bottle, visible only from the air.

These advertising campaigns have been so successful that Absolut annual sales have grown from ten thousand cases in the first year of the campaign to 7.3 million cases today. All by looking good.

Applying the principle

In sales, this principle applies to two main categories: personal appearance and the materials you hand out.

Let's start with you. You're already the best dressed and groomed person in your neighborhood. But could you look even better? If you say maybe, I'm sure family and friends will have lots of suggestions.

Now take a hard look at the handouts and sales materials you plan to use in your next few meetings. If someone handed these materials to you, would you say: "Wow, those sure look good"? If not, what can you do to present more professional materials?

Does your company provide additional materials that you could use?

Do you create your own slide presentations? In the age of digital photos, there is simply no excuse for a presentation that is all words. Words are boring. Go to your company's website, and your competitors' websites. See all the pictures? That's what you need to add. It's OK if they are gratuitous and maybe even a little irrelevant. As long as they look good.

You might be able to use your own digital snapshots, especially if you're selling homes or used office furniture. But you should also consider professional photos.

You may be surprised at all the choices you'll find if you search the web for "free clip art" and "free photos." And if you're willing to spend a few dollars, the choices can quickly become overwhelming.[213]

But make sure you start looking at a time when it's OK to get distracted for a few hours. Because I guarantee you will get distracted. It's just too much fun.

Reminders

- Remind yourself: looks matter.
- Examine each and every item used in the sales effort and ask: Is this the best I can do within my budget?
- Upgrade your slide presentations and handouts with professional photos.

Ask yourself

- What is the least attractive document I hand out?
- How could it be improved?
- What cost-effective actions could I take to insure that every document I hand out is as attractive as possible?
- Should I add photos to my materials and presentations?

> *"You do twenty-five different things,*
> *and one of them might work."*
> *— J. P. Plunkett*

Chapter **26**

Don't stop

Some people treat advertising and sales as isolated events, one-time occurrences. Those people are making a big mistake. The most successful programs don't stop with a single event. They go on, and on, and on.

The Charmin paper company was founded in 1928 in Green Bay, Wisconsin. According to a 1956 print ad, their toilet tissue was "softer than moonbeams, more gentle than dew."[214] But they didn't have much money to advertise, so few people knew that. In 1957, Procter & Gamble bought Charmin and the big money people looked for a better way to package this message.

One late night brainstorming session was held at a conference table stacked high with toilet tissue. The table was surrounded by people making no progress, and feeling the softness of toilet paper rolls. Finally, someone yelled in frustration, "Stop squeezing the Charmin."

Eureka! People squeeze melons and tomatoes at supermarkets. What if they squeezed the toilet tissue?

The ads were to be built around an irritable grocery employee. Some lawyer said that the ad had to use the name of an actual Procter & Gamble employee, so they searched employee rosters for "any name that had a wimpy, prissy sound to it."[215] George Whipple from the public relations department was paid a dollar for the use of his name.

In the script for the first ad, Mr. Whipple was so mean that he ran around the store grabbing toilet tissue from shoppers. Actor Dick Wilson humanized the image by having Mr. Whipple sneak a squeeze of his own.

"Please don't squeeze the Charmin" became a national catch phrase, and by 1969 it was the best selling toilet tissue in the land. By 1978, George Whipple was the third best known American.[216] Mr. Whipple's image has continued to soften, and the campaign continues to the present day. In part because the ads never stopped.

Procter & Gamble's commitment to continuous advertising goes back over a century. The company was founded in Cincinnati[217] in 1837 when candle maker William Procter merged his company with soap maker James Gamble.[218] Procter took over sales and Gamble handled operations, a split which the families continued through several generations of growth.

Their big break came after the Civil War when an employee accidentally left the soap mixing machine on for too long, and produced a "soap that floats." While listening to the Forty-fifth Psalm's reference to "ivory palaces" one Sunday, Harley Procter decided to rename "White Soap" as "Ivory Soap." He was so devout that he had to wait until Monday to share this idea with Gamble. They devoted the then unbelievable sum of $11,000 to advertising. In December 1882, they introduced the slogan "99 and 44/100ths percent pure," which is still used today.[219]

The campaign was a huge success, and reinforced top management's commitment to advertising. Procter & Gamble's advertising led to the success of Crisco cooking oil in 1911, Tide laundry detergent in 1947, and Crest toothpaste in 1955. Procter & Gamble is now considered "the biggest and most powerful advertiser in the world,"[220] and offers market-dominating products for every stage of the life cycle, from Pampers to Metamucil.

This top management commitment to advertising has led to enormous financial success and a product list that reads like an advertising hall of fame, including Mr. Clean, Cheer, Noxzema, Cover Girl, Oil of Olay, Folger's coffee, Hawaiian Punch, Secret, and Pepto Bismol. They just won't stop.

Applying the principle

Customers buy from people they like and have a relationship with. And according to Jim Cathcart in the book *Relationship Selling*, "The way to recognize a true sales professional is to look at what he or she does *after* the sale."[221]

In every industry, it is far more expensive to win business from a new client than from an old one. Even if your product is not in this year's budget, next year's budget is just twelve months away, or less. Cathcart's book offers many tips for keeping in touch, starting with taking responsibility for installing your product. And if the product does not need to be installed, make something up.

For example, he suggests that a real estate professional could prepare an "owners manual" for a new home, including locations of the power, gas, and water shutoffs, a list of important local phone numbers, and a map showing schools and stores. Or an insurance agent could prepare a policy summary which includes useful information to file away today, and looks ahead to insurance needs in the future.

He also suggests keeping in touch with everything from clipped magazine articles to handwritten notes, and a regular account review to uncover both satisfaction and dissatisfaction. Publicize the positive, and fix the negative.

And when you lose a sale, keep in touch with those people too. If you find ways to help people, they will remember you, they will come back to you, they will tell their friends, and sooner or later some of them will buy.

The key to relationship selling is don't stop. Look past today's victories and losses, and focus on building relationships that will be the foundation of your long-term success.

And on the inevitable days when progress feels slow, give yourself a pep talk about the fact that sales is a numbers game. If you knock on enough doors saying the right thing, your share will open.

Troy Waugh calls this the need to "succeed by failing more." "All advertising, public relations and direct mail programs have failure rates (nonresponse) that exceed ninety-five percent. But the one to five percent success can create excellent leads and pay for all your efforts."[222]

Reminders

- Accept the fact that promotion is not easy, and there is no magic bullet You just need to keep working away at it, using as many different techniques as you can think of.
- Find excuses to keep in touch by email, such as a running in-joke about the local baseball team or the state of the economy.
- Send handwritten notes often, and make sure that people know that you care.
- When someone helps you, thank them repeatedly – you cannot say thank you enough.
- Keep in touch after you win, and after you lose.
- For large customers, consider organizing a formal follow-up campaign:
    - Start by defining the precise objective, and setting a budget – both time and money.
    - Write a one-page plan for the next three months, including the objective, how you will measure success, estimates of any resources required, and their source.
    - Get off to a good start: Execute the first few activities with enthusiasm and verve.

- Test everything over and over. Try each element out on one or two people before sending it to ten people or a hundred.
- Monitor results of each campaign, so that you can repeat the things that work, and drop the things that don't.
- Set aside time every week to read books on sales. One good idea will pay for the book many times over.
- Remind yourself one more time: sales and marketing are not one time events, they are lifetime pursuits.

Ask yourself

- Analyze a recent sale: What happened afterwards? Did I plan clear follow-up? Did I do it?
- Do I make sure clients are happy after the sale, so they will keep coming back for more?
- With satisfied clients, do I collect data to prove it?
- Do I ask satisfied customers for referrals to others?
- If a client has problems after the sale, do I help solve them quickly enough to satisfy the client and save the relationship?

A final thought

"Nothing in the world can take the place of persistence.

Talent will not; nothing is more common than unsuccessful men with talent.

Genius will not; unrewarded genius is almost a proverb.

Education will not; the world is full of educated derelicts.

Persistence and determination are omnipotent.

The slogan 'press on' has solved and always will solve the problems of the human race."

– Calvin Coolidge

Quotations

Chapter 1: Attract attention - Harry in the film *Dumb and Dumber* - www.quotegeek.com

Chapter 2: Engage your customers - Philip Dormer Stanhope, 4th Earl Chesterfield - www.bartleby.com

Chapter 3: Appeal to self-interest - Travis Bickle in the film *Taxi Driver* - www.quotegeek.com

Chapter 4: Enhance value - Ralph Waldo Emerson - www.bartleby.com

Chapter 5: Listen - Dalai Lama - www.listen.org

Chapter 6: Test early and often - 1 Thessalonians – *The New Testament*

Chapter 7: Be optimistic and credible - Teddy Roosevelt - www.quotationspage.com

Chapter 8: Be creative - Scott Adams - www.quotationspage.com

Chapter 9: Stimulate curiosity - Ellen Parr - www.quotationspage.com

Chapter 10: Ask for help - Chinese proverb - www.bartleby.com

Chapter 11: Build consensus - Stella Blum - www.bartleby.com

Chapter 12: Personalize and customize - *The Simpsons* - www.quotegeek.com

Chapter 13: Quote testimonials - Basketball player Charles Barkley in testimonial ad for Nike - Berger, Warren. *Advertising Today*. New York: Phaidon, 2001, p. 279.

Chapter 14: Use a slogan - Johan Huizinga - www.bartleby.com

Chapter 15: Build on the brand - Old marketing joke - Twitchell, James B. *Twenty Ads that Shook the*

World: The Century's Most Groundbreaking Advertising and How It Changed Us All. New York: Crown, 2000.

Chapter 16: Repeat the message - Roland Barthes - www.bartleby.com

Chapter 17: Make a good first impression - Christoper Marlowe - Bartlett, John (Justin Kaplan ed.) *Bartlett's Familiar Quotations*, 17th ed. USA: Little, Brown, 2002.

Chapter 18: Tell a story - Hannah Arendt - www.quotationspage.com

Chapter 19: Dramatize the dull - Alfred Hitchcock - www.bartleby.com

Chapter 20: Write powerful headlines - Karl Kraus - www.bartleby.com

Chapter 21: Less is more - Voltaire - *Bartlett's Familiar Quotations*

Chapter 22: Make people happy - Oscar Wilde - www.bartleby.com

Chapter 23: Be cautious with humor - Mark Salzman, *Iron & Silk.* New York: Vintage Books, 1986, p. 37.

Chapter 24: Require immediate action - Captain Renault in the film *Casablanca* - www.quotegeek.com

Chapter 25: Look good - Jean Kerr - www.quotationspage.com

Chapter 26: Don't stop - Real estate broker J. P. Plunkett - *Boston Globe*, September 16, 2004, p. A4.

Notes

Introduction

1. Many observers have noted that "a lot of sales books say the same thing," despite the fact that few quote each other, or even mention that other systems exist. We take the position that every sales book can help some people, some of the time, and they are all worth reading sooner or later. AdverSelling can help you figure out where to start. And if even one good idea helps you close a sale, it will easily pay for the book and the time you spend reading.

2. "Rebuilding Profitable Business: The 2004 Miller Heiman Sales Effectiveness Study" Executive Summary, p. 4, available from www.millerheiman.com.

3. Smith, B. & Rutigliano, T. *Discover Your Sales Strengths*. USA: Warner Books, 2004, p. 24.

4. Ibid, p. 8.

5. Buckingham, Marcus and Donald Clifton. *Now, Discover Your Strengths*. New York: Free Press, 2001.

6. Ibid, p. 12.

7. Ibid, p. 78.

8. Bossidy, Larry, Ram Charan and Charles Burck. *Execution*. New York: Crown Business, 2002.

9. Meyers, David G. *Social Psychology*. 5th ed. New York: McGraw Hill, 1996, p. 49.

10. Miller, K.I. and P.R. Monge, "Participation, Satisfaction and Productivity. A Meta-Analytic review." *Academy of Management Review*, Vol. 29, 1986, p. 727-753.

Chapter 1 Attract attention

11. There are many estimates of the number of ads that Americans see each day. The numbers vary, but all agree that it is a lot. The three thousand per day number is quoted in Krumroy, Robert E. *Identity Branding*. Greensboro, NC: Lifestyles Press, 2000, p. xviii.

12. Baker, Stephen. "The Online Ad Surge," *Business Week*, November 22, 2004, p. 76.

13. Vranica, Susan and Steinberg, Brian. "The feathers did fly," *Wall Street Journal*, December 20, 2004, B6.

14. Lyman, Peter and Hal R. Varian, "How Much Information." www.sims.berkeley.edu/how-much-info.

15. To come up with this number, I assumed he spent one minute at each of the 42.8 million web domains, and that he never slept or took a break. I also assumed that everyone on the planet had agreed to freeze the web until his review was complete.

16. "Communications Blitz More Overwhelming for E-Business Workers Than Traditional Workers." *Pitney Bowes Online.* www.pb.com/cgi-bin/pb.dll/editorials/pb_press_release_ editorial.jsp?groupCatName=Our+Company&oid=8783&groupOID= 8004&locale=US&language=ENG>.

17. Albrecht, Karl. "The True Information Survival Skills." *TD* February 2001, p. 28-29.

18. Presentation by Tom Snyder, Huthwaite, ISA Conference, Washington DC, October 22, 2004, "Why prospecting messages fail and what you can do about it." See also the white paper "Prospecting for the Major Sale" at www.huthwaite.com.

Chapter 2 Engage your customers

19. However, it's probably been a few years since you got an envelope that said "You may already be a winner". In 2000, Publishers Clearinghouse agreed to pay $18.3 million to twenty-four states to settle lawsuits regarding deceptive practices, including misrepresenting how close a person is to winning. See for example the press release "State Reaches Settlement with Publishers Clearinghouse." www.atg.wa.gov/releases/rel_publishers_082200.html.

20. "Publishers Clearinghouse celebrates 50 years." www.pch.com/infocenter/consumeraffairs/news/news030403.shtml.

21. Trout, Jack. *Trout on Strategy.* USA: McGraw-Hill, 2004, p. 1.

22. Ries, Al & Trout, Jack. *Positioning: How to be seen and heard in the overcrowded marketplace.* USA: McGraw-Hill, 2001.

23. Smith, B. & Rutigliano, T. p.142.

24. Ibid, p.145.

25. Ibid, p.144.

Chapter 3 Appeal to self-interest

26. Fujinaka, Mariko. "Your Way." Riggs, Thomas, ed. *Encyclopedia of Major Marketing Campaigns.* Farmington, MI: Gale Group, 2000, p. 208-9.

27. Knight, Judson. "Grace Campaign." Riggs p. 802.
28. My mother sometimes bragged that Charles Atlas was a neighbor when she grew up in Richmond Hill, New York. She knew him as Angelo Siciliano.
29. Knight, "Mac Campaign." Riggs p. 287.
30. Ibid, p. 287.
31. The Daisy commercial was run during the NBC Monday night movie on September 7, 1964: *David and Bathsheba*, starring Gregory Peck and Susan Hayward.
32. Knight, "Daisy Campaign." Riggs p. 470.
33. Meyers p. 39.
34. Ibid, p. 59.
35. Bosworth, Michael T. *Solution Selling*. USA: McGraw-Hill, 1995, p. xxii.
36. Bosworth, p. 73.
37. Page, Rick. *Hope is Not a Strategy: – The 6 Keys to Winning the Complex Sale*. Atlanta GA: Nautilus Press, 2002, p. 60.

Chapter 4 Add value

38. Stanfel, Rebecca. "Intel Inside Campaign." Riggs p. 790.
39. Ibid, p. 794.
40. Cobau, Sally. "A Diamond Is Forever Campaign." Riggs p. 454.
41. Ibid, p. 450-1.
42. Ibid, p. 450.
43. Kanfer, Stefan. *The Last Empire: De Beers, Diamonds, and the World*. New York: Farrar Straus Giroux, 1993, p. 271.
44. Ibid, p. 341.
45. Cobau p. 455.
46. Fox, Stephen. *The Mirror Makers: A History of American Advertising and Its Creators*. USA: Vintage Books, 1985, p. 192.
47. Rackham, Neil. *SPIN Selling*. USA: McGraw-Hill, 1988, p. 8.
48. Wilson, Larry with Wilson, Hersch. *Stop Selling, Start Partnering*. New York: Wiley, 1994, p. 181.

Chapter 5 Listen

49. Covey, Stephen. *The Seven Habits of Highly Effective People*. New York: Free Press, 1990.
50. Goleman, Daniel, Richard Boyatzis and Annie McKee. *Primal Leadership*. Boston: Harvard Business School Press, 2002.

51. Purdy, Michael. "The Listener Wins," http://featuredreports.monster.com/listen/overview/ 15 April 2004.
52. Listening fifty percent of the time is recommended by Linda Richardson in *Stop Telling, Start Selling*, USA: McGraw-Hill, 1998, p. 189. The seventy percent recommendation comes from Deep, Sam and Sussman, Lyle. *Close the Deal*, Sandler Sales Institute. Cambridge, Mass: Perseus Books, 1999, p. 179.
53. Tracy, Brian. *Advanced selling strategies*. New York: Simon & Schuster, 1995, p. 133.
54. Daley, Kevin with Wolfe, Emmett. *Socratic Selling: How to Ask the Questions that Get the Sale. USA: McGraw-Hill, 1996.*

Chapter 6 Test early and often

55. Coleman, Ray. *The Man Who Made the Beatles*. New York: McGraw Hill, 1989, p. 97.
56. For example, Chapter 8 discusses a famous ad headline written by David Ogilvy: "At sixty miles an hour, the loudest noise in this new Rolls Royce comes from the electric clock." In his biography, Ogilvy says that he tested and rejected one hundred three other headlines before approving that one.
57. Amorosino, Chris John. "To Men." Riggs 1380.
58. Gladwell, Malcom, *The Tipping Point*. Boston: Little, Brown and Company, 2000, p. 258.
59. Ibid, p. 106.
60. Rackham p. 16.
61. Hassett, James, Albert Ingram, Matthew Hassett, and Emily Marino, "What Do Learners Like?: Ratings of Off-the-Shelf Web-Based Training Courses," *International Journal on E-Learning*. January-March 2003, 50-60.
62. Credit should go to Tom Snyder of Huthwaite for the idea that "sales is not a science experiment."
63. Nielsen, Jakob. *Designing Web Usability*. Indianapolis, IN: New Riders Publishing, 2000. Nielsen performed a number of studies to see how many testers were needed to identify problems with web pages. He concluded that seventy percent of the errors could be identified by using only three testers, and thirty percent with just one.

Chapter 7 Be optimistic and credible

64. McMath, Robert M., and Thom Forbes. *What Were They Thinking? Marketing Lessons I've Learned from over 80,000 New-Product Innovations and Idiocies.* New York: Random, 1998, p. 28.
65. Peterson, C., Seligman, M.E.P. & Vaillant, G.E. "Pessimistic explanatory style is a risk factor for physical illness: A thirty-five-year longitudinal study." *Journal of Personality and Social Psychology,* 1988, 55, p. 23-27.
66. Meyers p. 84.
67. Ibid p. 47.
68. Pratkanis, Anthony, and Elliot Aronson. *Age of Propaganda: The Everyday Use and Abuse of Persuasion.* Rev. ed. New York: Freeman, 2001, p. 162.
69. Meyers p. 278.
70. Ruvolo, A & Markus, H. "Possible selves and performance: The power of self-relevant imagery." *Social Cognition,* 1992, 9, p. 95-124.
71. Pratkanis and Aronson p. 122.
72. Ibid p. 122-3.
73. Friedman, Walter A. *Birth of a Salesman.* Cambridge, MA: Harvard University Press, 2004, p. 48.
74. Grant wrote his memoirs while dying from cancer to help his family recover from bankruptcy, caused by fraud committed by his brokerage firm partner.
75. Seligman, M. P. *Authentic Happiness: Using the New Positive Psychology to Realize Your Potential for Lasting Fulfillment.* New York: Free Press, 2002.
76. Gitomer, Jeffrey. *The Patterson Principles of Selling.* New Jersey: John Wiley, 2004, p. 54.
77. Friedman p. 136.
78. Seligman, Martin E. P. *Learned Optimism: How to Change Your Mind and Your Life.* New York: Free Press, 1998.

Chapter 8 Be creative

79. Garfield, Bob. "Top 100 Advertising Campaigns of the Century." *Advertising Age.* Advertising Age had three criteria for rating the ads: "1) If it was a watershed, discernibly changing the culture of advertising or the popular culture as a whole . . . . 2) If it itself was credited with creating a category, or if by its efforts a brand became

entrenched in its category as No. 1 . . . . 3) If it was simply unforgettable."

80. Hutchens, Patrick. "Honesty Campaign." Riggs p. 1893.

81. Ibid, p. 1896.

82. Ibid, p. 1896.

83. Ibid, p. 1897.

84. Legend has it that upon first hearing this line, one senior Rolls executive said: "We really must do something to improve our clock."

85. Amorosino, "Rolls-Royce." Riggs p. 1543.

86. Ibid, p. 1547.

87. Also see the webpage www.idea-engineering.com.

88. Other guides to creativity include Tom Wujec's *Five Star Mind: Games and Exercises to Stimulate Your Creativity and Imagination.* New York: Main Street Books, 1995, and *Wow! How did they think of that?* by Ted Coulson and Alison Strickland. Seminole, FL: Applied Creativity, Inc., 2000.

Chapter 9 Stimulate curiosity

89. Mack, Deborah. "Does She Campaign." Riggs p. 305.

90. Ibid p. 307.

91. Polykoff, Shirley. *Does She...Or Doesn't She?: And How She Did It.* New York: Doubleday, 1975, p. 34.

92. Mack, "Does She Campaign." Riggs p. 306.

93. Knight, "Burma Shave." Riggs p. 60-2.

94. The exact link is www.ebri.org/findings/ret_findings.htm.

95. It would have gone even faster if I hadn't gotten distracted by that article about retiring in Australia.

Chapter 10 Ask for help

96. Lawter, William Clifford. *Smokey Bear 20252: A Biography.* Alexandria, VA: Lindsay Smith Publishers, 1994.

97. Ibid.

98. Burg, Bob. *Endless Referrals.* USA: McGraw-Hill, 1999, p. 22, p. 7

99. Smith, B. & Rutigliano, T., p. 178.

Chapter 11 Build consensus

100. Many other techniques were also used to sell war bonds, notably celebrity auctions. Albert Einstein raised $100,000

auctioning original documents for the theory of relativity, and Lana Turner raised $5,200,000 by selling kisses. (Schnakenberg, Robert. "Buy War Bonds." Riggs p. 1853.)

101. Schnakenberg. "Just Say No." Riggs p. 860.
102. Miller, Robert B. & Heiman, Stephen E. *Strategic selling.* New York: Warner Books, 1985, p. 209. For an update of the approach, see Heiman, Stephen E and Sanchez, Diane *The New Strategic Selling: The Unique Sales System Proven Successful by the World's Best Companies, Revised and Updated for the 21st Century.* USA: Warner Business Books, 1998.

Chapter 12 Personalize and customize

103. Lipton, Ronnie. *Designing Across Cultures.* Cincinnati, OH: F&W Publications, Inc., 2002.
104. Hartman, Carl. "Targeting in Native Tongues." *The Washington Times* 29 August 2002. p. 11-17.
105. "2002 Fact Pack: A Handy Guide to the Advertising Business." *Advertising Age.* www.adage.com/news.cms?newsId=35696, p. 32.
106. *Business Week*, March 15, 2004, p. 68.
107. Mallett, Daryl F. "Tommy Hilfiger." Riggs p. 1768.
108. Ibid, p. 1770.
109. Baker, p. 79.
110. Richardson.

Chapter 13 Quote testimonials

111. The George Foreman Lean Mean Grilling Machine is available in small, medium, and large, wherever fine appliances are sold. Along with the George Foreman Indoor/Outdoor Electric Bar-B-Que Grill, George Foreman Grill Pan, George Foreman Party Grill, and the Big George Rotisserie. For more details, and for George's Doctrine of Love audio, see www.biggeorge.com.
112. The George Foreman Signature Collection is more than just supersized tuxedos, dress pants, and sports coats. The George Foreman Comfort Zone sets new standards for expanding waistlines and collars.
113. Pratkanis and Aronson p. 129.
114. Cialdini, Robert B. *Influence: Science and Practice.* 4th ed. Needham Heights, MA: Allyn & Bacon, 2001, p. 187.
115. *Fortune* magazine, June 22, 1998.

116. Hornstein, H.A., Fisch, E. & Holmes, M. "Influence of a model's feeling about his behavior and his relevance as a comparison other on observers' helping behavior." *Journal of Personality and Social Psychology,* 10, 1968, p. 222-226.

117. Mclean, Jacqueline A. "Hidden Camera Campaign." Riggs p. 1441.

118. *Advertising Age.* "The 20 Most Effective TV Ads of 2002." December 30, 2002.

119. Schnakenberg, "Ronco Campaign." Riggs p. 1552.

120. He did not, however, invent the "Bass-o-Matic" fish cleaner – that was Dan Aykroyd on *Saturday Night Live.*

Chapter **14** Use a slogan

121. Baue, William D. "We Try." Riggs p. 130.

122. Ibid.

123. Ibid.

124. Thanks to Bill Avril for this example.

Chapter **15** Build on the brand

125. Condry, Nancy. "Holiday Campaign." Riggs p. 340.

126. Ibid, p. 338-41.

127. "The Best Global Brands." *Business Week* 5 August 2002, p. 69.

128. Fujinaka, "Harley Davidson." Riggs p. 716.

129. Ibid, p. 717.

130. Aaker, David. *Managing Brand Equity.* New York: Free Press, 1991.

131. Rowland, Christopher. Drug ads deliver a few side effects: Firms reap rewards, but so do their rivals, and patients take data to the doc, study finds. *The Boston Globe,* June 12, 2003.

132. "Lessons from the Vioxx Fiasco," *Business Week,* November 29, 2004, p. 42.

133. *Business Week.* March 22, 2004, p. 98.

134. Ibid, p.99.

135. Twitchell, James. *Living It Up*: *America's Love Affair with Luxury.* New York: Simon & Schuster, 2002.

136. Krumroy p. 165.

137. Ibid, p. 165.

Chapter **16** Repeat the message

138. Twitchell, James B. *Twenty Ads that Shook the World: The Century's Most Groundbreaking Advertising and How It Changed Us All*. New York: Crown, 2000, p. 149.
139. Fox p. 188.
140. Aaker p. 160.
141. Pratkanis and Aronson p. 181.
142. Ibid, p. 182.
143. The famous slogan "think" which is forever linked to IBM and Watson was actually first used at National Cash Register, "apparently at Watson's suggestion," according to Walter Friedman in *Birth of a Salesman*, p. 150.
144. Ibid, p 138.

Chapter **17** Make a good first impression

145. Ries, Al. p. 43.
146. Ibid, p. 21.
147. Laidman, Jenni. "Making an Impression. 30 Seconds: Researcher Says Initial Contact Proves to Be the Image that Lasts in Person's Mind." *The Topeka Capital-Journal* 25 June 2001.
148. Knight, "Beatles." Riggs p. 251.
149. The sixty thousand requests for Beatles tickets easily beat the previous record of seven thousand for an Elvis Presley show.
150. Knight, "Beatles" Riggs p. 252.
151. Lampton, Bill, Ph.D. "How To Make A Strong First Impression: Seven Tips That Really Work." *Business Know-How.* www.businessknowhow.com/marketing/seventips.htm.
152. Lampton quotes this definition of a bore: "Somebody who talks about himself so much that you don't get to talk about yourself."

Chapter **18** Tell a story

153. Knight, "They Laughed." Riggs p. 1791.
154. Garfield, Bob. "Top 100 Advertising Campaigns of the Century." *Advertising Age.* www.adage.com/century/campaigns.html, pars. 30 and 40.
155. Caples, John. *Tested Advertising Methods*. Rev. Fred E. Hahn. 5th ed. New Jersey: Prentice, 1997, p. xviii. Although the advertising world celebrated Caples's talents, his mother was less

impressed. When he went home for Christmas dinner and showed
her the ads, she asked questions like: Can people really learn to
play the piano by mail? She did not seem proud of a son whose ads
stretched the truth and said, "You'd better not let your father see
this."
156. Ibid.
157. Walters, Lilly. *Secrets of Superstar Speakers*. USA: McGraw-
Hill, 2000, p. 94.

Chapter **19** Dramatize the dull

158. Ogilvy says the eye patch was his whim. One day as he headed
to the studio for a photo shoot: "I ducked into a drugstore and
bought an eye patch for $1.50. Exactly why it turned out to be so
successful, I shall never know." But Edith Jette, the wife of
Hathaway's president, claims it was her idea: she told her husband
that eye-patch wearing men had a mysterious sense of distinction,
and he gave the idea to Ogilvy. Twitchell, *Twenty Ads.* p. 141.
159. Ibid p. 142.
160. Stanfel, "Pepsi Campaign." Riggs p. 1337. Despite the success
of this approach, some at Pepsi felt the commercials were too
abrasive. In 1984 the campaign was replaced by Michael Jackson
explaining in song why Pepsi was "The Choice of a New
Generation."
161. Pratkanis and Aronson p. 172.
162. Ibid, p. 173.
163. Ibid, p. 177.
164. According to www.cunard.com, the Empire State lying on its
side is only 110 feet longer than the Queen Mary 2.

Chapter **20** Write powerful headlines

165. Caples p. 14.
166. Amorosino, "Phoenix." Riggs p. 1378.
167. Schrello, Don M. *How to Market Training and Information.*
USA: Schrello Direct Marketing, 1994, p. 12-7.
168. Parinello, Anthony. *Selling to VITO the Very Important Top
Officer*, Second edition. Holbrook, MA: Adams Media Corporation,
1999, p. 58.
169. Caples p. 133.

Chapter 21 Less is more

170. Joyce, Alan. "Advertising in the 1990s Campaign." Riggs p. 744-6.

171. Americans also open their refrigerators over one billion times every single day, looking for something to eat.

172. Jesse White played the lonely Maytag repairman from 1967 until he retired in 1989. He was replaced by Gordon Jump, better known as Arthur "Big Guy Carlson," the station manager on the show "WKRP in Cincinnati." Jump retired shortly before his death in 2003 and was replaced by Hardy Rawls, a former Mister Goodwrench.

173. Risland, Susan. "Lonely Maytag Repairman Campaign." Riggs p. 1018-23.

174. Coryell, Anita Louise. "You Press the Button, We Do the Rest Campaign." Riggs p. 528.

175. Ironically, in the last few years the mail-in camera has again became one of Kodak's most successful products, as digital photography has destroyed the film-based business.

176. Coryell p. 528.

177. Ibid, p. 530.

178. The "80/20 rule" has been attributed to the nineteenth century Italian economist Vifredo Pareto, and there are many many variations, including "Eighty percent of your business comes from twenty percent of your customers," "Eighty percent of the work is done by twenty percent of the people" and "Eighty percent of all beer is consumed by twenty percent of the beer drinkers."

Chapter 22 Make people happy

179. Baue, William D. "Dedicated to Pleasure Campaign." Riggs p. 474.

180. Ibid, p. 474.

181. Condry. "Have a Coke." Riggs p. 333. During the filming of this commercial, Mean Joe couldn't have been nicer. The child actor was in complete awe and missed so many lines that it took three days to complete the shoot. Despite chugging eighteen Cokes in a single day, Joe remained good natured.

182. Ibid, p. 331.

183. Ibid, p. 332-3.

184 Seligman, Martin. *Authentic Happiness.*

185. Brickman, P., D. Coates, and R. Janoff-Bulman. "Lottery winners and accident victims: Is happiness relative?" *Journal of Personality and Social Psychology*, 1978, 36: 917-927.
186. Ibid, p. 47.
187. Ibid, p. 61.
188. Ibid, p. 52.
189. Seligman, Martin. *Learned Optimism: How to Change Your Mind and Your Life.*
190. I know that many people believe this because my desk is stuffed with free pens and post-it notes which I never use.
191. If you can figure out what the experts have in mind, please let me know. I'd like to order a few thousand of those myself.
192. Smith, B. & Rutigliano, T., p. 80.
193. Gitomer p. 83.

Chapter 23 Be cautious with humor

194. Joe Isuzu was played by character actor David Leisure, who also appeared in the 1980 comedy movie *Airplane* as a Hare Krishna begging for donations at the airport, and as the obnoxious neighbor Charley Dietz on NBC's early 90s sitcom *Empty Nest*.
195. Mack, "Frito Campaign." Riggs p. 594.
196. Noriega, Chon A. "There May Be a Frito Bandito in Your House." *San Diego Latino Film Festival Current Trends* 1997. www.sdlatinofilm.com/trends12.html.
197. Horovitz, Bruce. "Smile! You're the stars of the Super ad Bowl." www.usatoday.com/money/advertising/2003-01-24-sb03-animal-ad_x.htm.

Chapter 24 Require immediate action

198. Cialdini p. 62.
199. Ibid, p. 67.
200. Ibid, p. 71.
201. Rackham, p. 51.
202. *Ibid*, p. 44.
203. Schiffman, Stephan. *25 Sales Strategies That Will Boost Your Sales Today.* Avon, Massachusetts: Adams Media, 1999.
204. Ibid, p. 83.
205. Cialdini p. 65.

Chapter 25 Look good

206. Hassett, J., and K. White. *Psychology in Perspective*. New York: Harper & Row, 1984, p. 626.
207. Alsop, Ronald, and Bill Abrams. *The Wall Street Journal on Marketing*. Homewood: Dow Jones, 1986, p. 100.
208. Another survey from this source reported that consumers were most dissatisfied with the packaging of lunch meat (77%) and least dissatisfied with ketchup (34%). Perhaps surprising in light of Richard Armour's verse: "Shake and shake the ketchup bottle, none'll come, and then a lot'll."
209. Alsop p. 143.
210. "The Story," a 25-page document you can download from www.absolut.com, p. 11.
211. I doubt that I would be able to recognize the uneven qualities in the waters used by Absolut's competitors.
212. Ibid, p. 2.
213. Our favorite sources for paid photos include www.photos.com, www.gettyimages.com, and www.corbis.com. But be warned that free or paid, you'll need to learn a little about file sizes and types, not to mention copyrights.

Chapter 26 Don't stop

214. Fujinaka, "Don't Squeeze." Riggs p. 1433.
215. Ibid, p. 1436.
216. Ibid, p. 1436-7. Whipple's third place finish put him behind President Richard Nixon and Billy Graham.
217. Cincinnati was then known as "Porkopolis" because of its hog slaughtering industry, which produced an enormous amount of lye used to make soap and candles.
218. Rummel, Jack. "Aleve: All Day Strong, All Day Long Campaign." Riggs p. 1422.
219. Knight, "99 and 44/100%." Riggs p. 1418-21.
220. Fujinaka, "Don't Squeeze." Riggs p. 1433.
221. Cathcart, Jim. *Relationship Selling*. New York: Berkley Publishing Group, 1990, p. 100.
222. Waugh, Troy. *101 Marketing Strategies for Accounting, Law, Consulting, and Professional Services Firms*. New Jersey: John Wiley, 2004, p. 227.

Index

About the author

James Hassett founded LegalBizDev to help lawyers develop new business more quickly by applying best practices from other law firms and from other professions. Before he started working with lawyers, Jim had 20 years of experience as a sales trainer and consultant to companies from American Express to Zurich Financial Services. Jim has published seven books (including *Legal Business Development: A Step by Step Guide* and *The LegalBizDev Desk Reference*™) and more than seventy articles in publications ranging from the *New York Times Magazine* to *Legal Management* and *Strategies: The Journal of Legal Marketing.* He is a frequent speaker at regional and national conferences, including the New York, New England, and Southeastern chapters of the Legal Marketing Association. Jim has a Ph.D. from Harvard University, and is an Adjunct Associate Professor of Psychology at Boston University. His blog Legal Business Development (at www.jimhassett.com) was selected by *TechnoLawyer* as one of "the most influential legal blogs" and featured in *BlawgWorld 2007.* Jim also writes a monthly column for *Law Firm Inc.,* tracking the latest trends in business development.

26 AdverSelling™ Principles

The Top Six

Attract attention
Engage your customers
Appeal to self-interest
Add value
Listen
Test early and often

Your Attitude

Be optimistic and credible
Be creative
Stimulate curiosity
Ask for help
Build consensus

Your Presentations

Make a good first impression
Tell a story
Dramatize the dull
Write powerful headlines
Less is more

Your Message

Personalize and customize
Quote testimonials
Use a slogan
Build on the brand
Repeat the message

Your Actions

Make people happy
Be cautious with humor
Require immediate action
Look good
Don't stop